# Introduction

When the Moscow-based design team headed by Mikhail Leont'yevich Mil' was granted its own prototype manufacturing facility in Panki (Moscow Region) in the late 1940s and became OKB-329 (*opytno-konstrooktorskoye byuro* – experimental design bureau), it was in a position to bring out a long line of successful helicopters in various weight classes. The first of these was the three-seat GM-1 of 1949, which entered production as the Mi-1 (NATO reporting name *Hare*). The success achieved in the early 1950s with the Mi-4 *Hound* medium utility helicopter imbued the staff of OKB-329 with confidence and prompted them to try their hand at considerably heavier rotorcraft. The designers decided that their next product should be a helicopter capable of airlifting cargoes weighing some 6,000 kg (13,230 lb), such as heavy artillery pieces with their tractors and self-propelled guns for the airborne assault troops. They were aware that all previous attempts both at home and abroad to build a helicopter with an all-up weight in excess of 14 tonnes (30,870 lb) had ended in failure. Nevertheless, they set to work with a will, and in late 1952 the OKB drafted the first project of a huge helicopter tentatively designated **VM-6** – that is, *vertolyot Mil'a* (Mil' helicopter) with a payload of six tons.

Despite the opinion of many Soviet and foreign specialists who expressly recommended a tandem twin-rotor layout for heavy machines, Mikhail L. Mil' opted for a conventional single-rotor layout. He took the bold decision to start projecting a four-blade main rotor of a hitherto unseen diameter in excess of 30 m (98 ft). Moreover, for the first time in Soviet design practice The VM-6 was designed around a turboshaft engine – a single TV-2VM with a 5,500-shp take-off rating and a 4,700-shp nominal rating. This engine developed by OKB-19 under Chief Designer Pavel A. Solov'yov in Perm' was an adaptation of the 6,250-ehp TV-2F turboprop (a product of the Kuibyshev-based OKB-276 under Chief Designer Nikolay D. Kuznetsov) featuring a free turbine; this layout made it possible to adjust the main rotor RPM within a range that ensured maximum economic efficiency and the greatest possible operating radius.

Soon, however, the Soviet military posed a new specific operational requirement (SOR), demanding a 50% increase in the helicopter's payload. The OKB had to undertake a complete redesign; the second version of the VM-6 was considerably larger and powered by two TV-2VMs instead of one, the engines being located side by side ahead of the main gearbox. In addition, the SOR stipulated a maximum speed of 400 km/h (249 mph). This prompted the designers to consider the compound helicopter layout, which was in vogue at that time; the VM-6 was to feature detachable low-set cantilever wings of considerable span mounting two turboprop engines with tractor propellers at mid-span. The wings would off-load the main rotor in flight, allowing the helicopter to cruise at speeds comparable to those of fixed-wing transport aircraft.

The preliminary design project was ready by the end of 1953. On 11th June 1954 the Soviet Council of Ministers (= government) issued a directive officially sanctioning development of the giant helicopter, which was now known as the **V-6**, the V again standing for *vertolyot*. The machine was regarded as '*a new means of airlifting army units and almost all types of artillery pieces fielded at the army division level*' and was intended for carrying a 6,000-kg payload at the normal all-up weight, 8,000 kg (17,640 lb) in high gross weight configuration and 11,500 kg (25,360 lb) in a contingency over short distances.

A display model of the Mi-6's precursor – the VM-6 project (the later version with two TV-2VM turboshafts). Note the parabolic nose with a machine-gun, the four-blade main rotor and the low-set wings with additional turboprop engines for forward propulsion.

**Acknowledgements**
The book is illustrated with photos by Sergey Boordin, Yefim Gordon, Dmitriy Petrochenko, Sergey Popsuyevich, Andrey Zinchuk, Aidan Curley, Peter Davison, Martin Novak, ITAR-TASS, the Novosti Press Agency (APN), as well as from the archive of the Mil' Moscow Helicopter Plant, Rostvertol JSC, Russian Helicopters, the M. M. Gromov Flight Research Institute (LII), the personal archive of Yefim Gordon and from the following web sources: www.helikits.net, www.super-hobby.ru, www.modelist.zp.ua, www.scale-rotors.com, www.arcair.com, www.rumodelism.com, www.oldmodelkits.com, www.scalemates.com, www.familie-wimmer.com, www.modelsua.com, www.veb-plasticart.com, www.aviaforum.ru, www.litnik.in.ua, www.modellversium.de, www.hobby-modelist.ru. Line drawings by Andrey Yurgenson. Colour drawings by Viktor Mil'yachenko.

# The Mi-6 is Born

**B**y the end of 1954 the Mil' OKB had completed the advanced development project (ADP) for the V-6; N. G. Roosanovich was the project chief. Unlike the competing OKB-938 headed by Nikolay I. Kamov, which concurrently developed the Ka-22 compound helicopter of approximately the same class with two turboshaft engines installed at the tips of shoulder-mounted strut-braced wings to drive side-by-side rotors and tractor propellers, the Mil' OKB rejected the compound rotorcraft layout as economically inefficient, retaining only small wings. The latter were now shoulder-mounted and had variable incidence (with two settings – for normal flight and autorotation mode), creating enough lift to absorb up to 25% of the all-up weight in cruise flight.

The cavernous cargo cabin measuring 12 x 2.65 x 2.5 m (39 ft 4½ in x 8 ft 8⅜ in x 8 ft 2½ in) was similar in size to those of the Antonov An-8 *Camp* and An-12 *Cub* military transports. The stressed floor with tie-down cleats permitted transportation of heavy vehicles and cargoes. For example, the V-6 could carry two 57-mm ASU-57 self-propelled guns or a BTR-152 armoured personnel carrier, various guns and howitzers with their tractors, or engineer troops materiel. Detachable troop seats could be installed along the walls and on the centreline; in casualty evacuation (CASEVAC) configuration the helicopter could accommodate 41 stretcher cases and two medical attendants. (Jumping ahead of the story, in an emergency the helicopter has been known to carry as many as 150 persons.) A detachable external sling system ensured the carriage of slung loads weighing up to 8,000 kg (17,640 lb).

Engine power was distributed via the R-6 four-stage planetary main gearbox (R = *redooktor* – reduction gear) to the main and tail rotors, the gearbox cooling fan, generators, hydraulic pumps and other accessories. The R-6 could absorb a torque of as much as 60,000 kg-m (434,076 lb-ft); western engineers did not succeed in developing a main gearbox of comparable capacity until seven years later.

The biggest challenge facing the designers of the V-6 was the design of the main rotor blades, whose number was increased from four to five. The OKB developed all-metal blades of trapezoidal planform with a steel spar and a rib-and-stringer structure divided into sections (called pockets) which were not rigidly interconnected; this relieved the structure of considerable variable stresses as the blades flexed. For the first time in Soviet practice the rotor head incorporated hydraulic dampers. The four-blade tail rotor had wooden blades. The flight control system incorporated hydraulic actuators and an AP-31V three-channel autopilot borrowed from the Mi-4.

The wingless first prototype V-6 (Mi-6) with TV-2VM engines hovers at Zakharkovo airfield. Note the windowless front entry door and the dome-shaped navigator's glazing.

By 1st June 1955 the V-6 had passed the so-called mock-up review commission (a project analysis by the customer for the purpose of eliminating grave shortcomings at an early stage). Shortly afterwards plant No.329 in Panki and the production plant No.23 situated in Fili (then a western suburb but now long since part of Moscow) began manufacturing the first prototype of the helicopter which was now officially designated **Mi-6** and allocated the product code *iz**deli**ye* 50. (*Izdeliye* (product) such-and-such was, and still is, a commonly used code for designating Soviet/Russian military hardware items.)

The first prototype was assembled in the workshop at the now-defunct Zakharkovo airfield on the northern outskirts of Moscow (it was closed in 1962 and redeveloped by 1970). In October 1956 the machine was largely completed in the wingless version, with the exception of the main rotor, the manufacturing of which was lagging behind. For this reason the helicopter was fitted with an aerodynamic brake (moulinette, or 'club rotor') instead of the normal main rotor, and it was decided to conduct fatigue tests for the time being. Not until June of the following year was the rotor completed and installed; thus the fatigue test airframe was upgraded to flight test status.

On 5th June 1957 Mil' OKB project test pilot Rafail I. Kaprelyan performed the first hover in the Mi-6 at Zakharkovo; the first real flight (a circuit of the airfield) followed on 18th June. The flight tests continued well into the autumn, and on 30th October 1957 the Mi-6 established its first world record by lifting a payload of 12,004 kg (26,468.8 lb) to an altitude of 2,432 m (7,979 ft). This was twice the record figure attained previously by the Sikorsky S-56 heavy helicopter.

Front view of the first prototype, showing the asymmetric glazing of the navigator's station.

In February 1958 plant No.23 completed the second prototype, which had all the equipment stipulated by the project – the wings, the external sling system, the autopilot and so on. Both prototypes took part in the 1958 Aviation Day air display at Moscow-Tushino airfield. After that, the NATO's Air Standards Co-ordinating Committee (ASCC) allocated the reporting name *Hook* (H for helicopter) to the Mi-6.

Manufacturer's tests of the initial TV-2VM-powered version were completed in December 1958. Then, however, the OKB decided to re-engine the Mi-6 with all-new Solov'yov D-25V turboshafts derived from

Starboard side view of the first prototype Mi-6.

The second prototype V-6 (Mi-6) with D-25V engines and wings. No armament was fitted at this stage.

An early Mi-6 *sans suffixe* with a Mi-1 flying chase. The early-style tapered main rotor blades are clearly visible; note also the A-12.7 machine-gun under the nose.

**Opposite page:**
A still-uncoded Mi-6 built by the Rostov plant No.168 in 1962 (c/n 2681110V). The mainwheel spats and oleo fairings were soon eliminated from production Mi-6s

A Mi-6 *sans suffixe* built by the Moscow/Fili plant No.23 (c/n 1030302V). Neither the main gear fairings nor the machine-gun mount are fitted.

An uncoded Mi-6 seen prior to delivery; note the strake aerial along the starboard side and the Yagi aerial aft of the navigator's access door. The vehicle is an APA-2 ground power unit on a ZiL-164 chassis.

the core of the D-20P commercial turbofan. While having the same power rating as the TV-2VM, the new engine was shorter and lighter. However, the D-25V's free turbine turned in the opposite direction; hence a new R-7 main gearbox had to be designed. Plant No.23 completed the first D-25V-powered helicopter in the spring of 1959. Meanwhile, the state acceptance (= certification) trials of the Mi-6 at the Soviet Air Force State Research Institute named after Valeriy P. Chkalov (GK NII VVS – *Gosudarstvennyy krasnoznamyonnyy naoochno-issledovatel'skiy institoot voyenno-vozdooshnykh seel*) were begun with the old TV-2VM engines in the summer of 1959 in order to save time. When the D-25V-powered version joined the trials, the first machine returned to Zakharkovo for re-engining.

More world records were established on the Mi-6 just before and in the course of the state acceptance trials. For example, on 16th April 1959 the helicopter flew two missions captained by Sergey G. Brovtsev and Rafail I. Kaprelyan respectively, climbing to

5,584 m (18,321 ft) with a payload of 5 tons (11,025 lb) on the first occasion and to 4,885 m (16,028 ft) with a payload of 10 tons (22,050 lb) on the second. The high power/weight ratio and excellent aerodynamics enabled the Mi-6 to set a number of speed records as well. On 21st September 1961, captained by Nikolay V. Lyoshin, it reached a speed of 320 km/h (198.88 mph), which had long been regarded as unattainable for helicopters. For this achievement the American Helicopter Society awarded to the Mil' OKB the prestigious Sikorsky Prize. On 26th August 1964 a crew captained by Boris K. Galitskiy scored a still greater success; the Mi-6 clocked a speed of 340.15 km/h (211.4 mph) over a 100-km (62-mile) course. A total of 16 payload-to-altitude and speed records were established on the type between 1957 and 1964.

The Soviet Armed Forces were so much in need of heavy helicopters that the Mi-6 was ordered into production nearly two years before the completion of the state acceptance trials. The latter were accompa-

Another Moscow-built Mi-6 *sans suffixe* (c/n 1030402V) with external tanks attached.

Another view of the same helicopter with the starboard cowling partly open, the lower portions acting as work platforms. Note the Yagi aerials repositioned further forward.

A Moscow-built Soviet Air Force Mi-6 *sans suffixe* disgorges materiel; note the clamshell cargo door design typical of the early version (with large cut-outs for the vehicle loading ramps).

nied by a fair share of problems and took more than 18 months. For example, the D-25V engine was initially prone to surging, and test flights were performed in October 1960 specifically to assess the risk of surge and failure in flight. Tests of the external sling system, including emergency jettisoning of the cargo, were completed before the end of November 1961. Several well-known test pilots, including Gherman V. Alfyorov, Sergey G. Brovtsev, B. V. Zemskov, Rafail I. Kaprelyan, Gurghen R. Karapetyan, Vasiliy P. Koloshenko, Nikolay V. Lyoshin, Yegor F. Milyutichev *et al*, took part in the trials.

The state acceptance trials were successfully completed in December 1962. The GK NII VVS report stated: *'The prototype Mi-6 transport/troopship helicopter powered by two D-25V turboshafts is the biggest helicopter in the world and the first Soviet helicopter with turboshaft engines. It is superior to all Soviet helicopters in its performance and, above all, as regards the payload, dimensions of the cargo hold, the number of troops and the amount of combat materiel it can carry.'* In 1963 the Mi-6 was officially included into the inventory of the Armed Forces.

Here we have to go back in time a little. In 1959 plant No.168 in Rostov-on-Don joined the Mi-6 programme, manufacturing the first four production machines in that year. A branch office of the Mil' OKB was set up at plant No.168 for the purpose of perfecting the helicopter and developing new versions. in 1962, After completing just 50 Mi-6s, plant No.23 was transferred to the Ministry of General Machinery (MOM – *Ministerstvo* **ob**schchevo ma**shin**ostro**yen**iya) responsible for the Soviet space and missile programmes, producing rockets and spacecraft from then on. This left the Rostov plant as the sole manufacturer of the Mi-6. The production rate peaked in 1974 when 74 machines were delivered. A total of 874 Mi-6s in various versions had been built by plant No.168 when production ended in 1980, whereupon it was supplanted on the

Rostov assembly line by the Mi-26 new-generation helicopter (of which more will be said later). Thus, total Mi-6 production amounted to 924 copies.

Production Mi-6s differed from the prototypes in several respects. Notably, an NUV-1 gimballed mount (*noso**vaya** oosta**novk**a ver-to**lyot**naya* – nose [machine-gun] mount for helicopters) with a 12.7-mm (.50 calibre) Afanas'yev A-12.7 machine-gun was added under the navigator's station in the extreme nose, allowing the navigator to subdue any enemy opposition prior to a landing assault. Soon after production entry the original convex front transparency of the navigator's station gave place to an optically flat window eliminating annoying reflections and distortion. The mainwheel spats and the airfoil-section main gear oleo fairings were soon deleted as impractical.

The Mil' OKB kept refining the Mi-6. For example, new constant-chord main rotor blades featuring a one-piece tubular spar with variable-thickness walls and pockets with metal foil honeycomb filler were introduced into production in 1959-62; they were both stronger and less labour-intensive to manufacture. Shortly after the beginning of flight tests the original single-chamber main gear oleos were replaced by twin-chamber oleos featuring a fluid by-pass system connecting the two chambers; this design minimised the risk of ground resonance. In 1962 the adjustable wings gave place to fixed ones, which reduced weight and simplified the piloting technique; in the same year the AP-31V autopilot was replaced by the improved AP-34V and an Ivchenko AI-8 turbine auxiliary power unit (APU) was installed on the port clamshell door of the cargo hatch to facilitate engine starting. In 1963 the stabiliser structure was reinforced. In 1967 the helicopter was fitted with a main rotor speed governor. The service life of the helicopter's main units and assemblies (including the main rotor blades) was progressively increased from 50 hours in 1957 to 200

A Rostov-built Mi-6 *sans suffixe* manufactured in 1964 (c/n 4681606V) shows off the late-model constant-chord main rotor blades.

Smartly painted Mi-6 *sans suffixe* CCCP-06174 was the demonstrator of the commercial version lacking the machine-gun mount and the Yagi aerials typical of military examples. Note the heat shields on the wing roots.

Here CCCP-06174 has had chrome-plated hub caps added for its appearance at the 1965 Paris Air Show.

hours in 1961, 500 hours in 1965, 800 hours in 1969 and finally 1,500 hours in the 1970s.

We might also mention various improvements which were tested but did not make it into production. These included new main rotor blades with a steel spar and a glass-fibre secondary structure, four types of dust/debris filters for the Mi-6's engine air intakes enabling operation in dusty locations, an external sling system with a load-carrying capacity increased to 12 tons (26,460 lb) and so on.

A **commercial transport version** of the Mi-6 *sans suffixe* was developed in 1963 to meet a requirement placed by Aeroflot Soviet Airlines, which needed a heavy-lift chopper to support construction and oil/natural gas

drilling work in the eastern regions of the USSR. It differed from the basic military version in lacking the machine-gun mount and having some changes in the equipment. (It has to be said that the Mi-6 first entered service with civil operators in the Soviet Union in 1961, but these were presumably ex-military machines.) A Rostov-built demonstrator of the commercial version registered CCCP-06174 (c/n 5682010V – that is, year of manufacture 1965, plant No.168 (the first digit is omitted for security reasons), Batch 20, 10th and final helicopter in the batch, the meaning of the V suffix is not entirely clear) made the Mi-6's international debut at the 26th Paris Air Show in 1965 where it was one of the show-stealers. This version was built in quantity.

# Version Variety

The high performance and capacious cargo cabin of the Mi-6 allowed it to spawn numerous military and civil versions. This, the need to ensure the mobility of the Soviet missile forces led to the development of the **Mi-6PRTBV** (*podvizhnaya raketno-tekhnicheskaya baza vertolyotnovo tipa* – heliborne mobile missile maintenance base) intended for rapid redeployment of missiles and readying them for launch. It could transport to the launch sites the warheads of intercontinental ballistic missiles (ICBMs), or complete 8K11 and 8K14 intermediate-range ballistic missiles (IRBMs) and R-9 and R-10 theatre ballistic missiles without their launchers. Bearing no tactical code, the Mi-6PRTBV prototype (c/n 1030302V – that is, year of manufacture 19615, plant No.23 (03 is a code used for security reasons), Batch 03, 02nd helicopter of ten in the batch) entered flight test in 1960; two years later it was recommended for service but did not enter production.

The **Mi-6RVK** (*raketno-vertolyotnyy kompleks* – heliborne missile system) was co-developed by the Mil' OKB and enterprises of the Ministry of Medium Machinery (MSM – *Ministerstvo srednevo mashinostroyeniya*) responsible for the Soviet atomic industry in response to a Council of Ministers directive dated 5th February 1962. Apart from the helicopter itself, the system included the 9K53 *Loona-MV* (Moon) and 9K73 (alias R-17V) missile systems; these were heliborne versions of the 9M21 (NATO *FROG-7*) theatre ballistic missile and the 8K114 (SS-1 *Scud*) IRBM respectively with new lightweight SP launchers. The Mi-6RVK (c/n 2681110V) was successfully tested in 1963-65, but again no series production ensued because the system was deemed to be effective only in rare cases.

In 1962 an **electronic countermeasures (ECM) version** of the Mi-6 made its appearance; its mission was to protect the radars forming part of the country's air defence system from being detected by the enemy's electronic intelligence (ELINT) assets. The helicopter was fitted with appropriate mission equipment and could be identified by the additional aerials on the starboard side. Later, In the 1980s, the Mil' OKB developed the **Mi-6PP** (*postanovshchik pomekh* – ECM aircraft) intended for jamming the adversary's airborne early warning and control (AEW&C) assets and airborne ELINT systems. Neither of these two versions were built in series.

In 1958 the Mil' OKB started work on the **Mi-6M** (*morskoy* – maritime, or naval) shore-based anti-submarine warfare (ASW) heli-

The only known photo of the Mi-6PRTBV heliborne mobile missile maintenance base.

The one-off Mi-6RVK (c/n 2681110V) with a 9K53 *Loo-MV* missile on its mobile erector/launcher.

Here the Mi-6RVK is shown with a different missile – the 9K73, a heliborne version of the *Scud*.

**Right and below:** The Mi-6M experimental anti-submarine warfare helicopter with the large panniers accommodating four PLAT ASW torpedoes or *Kondor* missiles.

**Bottom:** Another shot of the Mi-6M in flight, with the doors of the weapons panniers open.

copter which was intended to carry four PLAT air-launched ASW torpedoes (*protivolodochnaya aviatsionnaya torpeda*) or *Kondor* (Condor) missiles in two large lateral panniers. The helicopter was built in 1963. In 1965 one more Mi-6 was converted under the *Boorlak* (barge hauler) programme into an ASW/mine countermeasures (MCM) helicopter designed to tow an experimental sonar or a mine clearing sled. (In 19th-century Russia, the *boorlaki* were teams of strongmen whose job was to haul barges up rivers by means of ropes, hence the name.) Development of the mission equipment took longer than expected, and the naval versions of the helicopter were not even submitted for state acceptance trials, finding use as testbeds for new ASW equipment.

In a more peaceful vein, the **Mi-6P** (*passazheerskiy* – passenger, used attributively) was developed in 1965. The comfortable passenger cabin was provided with large rectangular windows, heat- and soundproofing, coat stowage and a toilet; it accommodated 70 or 80 passengers five-abreast, depending on the seat pitch. The rear clamshell doors and cargo ramp were replaced by an identically shaped fairing which incorporated built-in airstairs on the centreline and the AI-8 APU. In case of need the Mi-6P could be easily configured for transport or CASEVAC duties. The prototype (CCCP-58647, c/n 6682905V) was unveiled at the 1967 Paris Air Show. The Mi-6P was not built in series either; the prototype was transferred to the Soviet Air Force on 12th May 1970.

The **Mi-6PS** (*poiskovo-spasahtel'nyy* – search and rescue, used attributively) was developed in 1966 for locating and retrieving the crews of Soviet manned spacecraft, as well as the re-entry capsules, after their landings. It had additional avionics facilitating overwater navigation (in case the capsule splashed down somewhere in the ocean after an emergency de-orbiting instead of landing in a designated area of Kazakhstan), a cabin with medical equipment for the cosmonauts' rehabilitation after returning to the conditions of normal gravity, an external sling system for transporting the capsule, a rescue hoist, rubber dinghies and life rafts. The prototype (c/n 2681006V) was converted by the Air Force's 535th ARZ (*aviaremontnyy zavod* – aircraft repair plant) in Konotop (Soomy Region, the Ukraine) in January 1969.

In 1967 the Mil' OKB brought out the **Mi-6PZh** water bomber version (*pozharnyy* – fire-fighting). It had the wings deleted to save weight and improve hovering performance. a tank holding 12 tons (26,460 lb) of water and a tank for a foaming agent were installed in the cabin, discharging through a nozzle passing through the external sling hatch; twin tubular booms hinged at the

**Above:** A model of the Mi-6P heli-liner with rectangular cabin windows displayed in 1965.

**Above:** The sole prototype of the Mi-6P, CCCP-58647, at the Mil' OKB's flight test facility. Note the 1967 Le Bourget exhibit code H-239.

**Below:** Two views of CCCP-58647 seen in the static park at the Moscow-Domodedovo airshow on 9th July 1967.

**This page:** CCCP-06174 after conversion as the ill-fated Mi-6PZh waterbomber prototype and repaint in a red/white colour scheme. Here it is seen dumping water during a demo flight. Note the absence of wings – a weight-saving measure.

This excellent shot of the Mi-6PZh shows the centrally located water discharge nozzle.

Another view of Mi-6PZh CCCP-06174. Note the ventral articulated tubes for water replenishment at the hover.

**Opposite page:** '41 Yellow' (c/n 9683901V), the prototype of the improved Mi-6PZh-2 waterbomber equipped with a water cannon under the nose, is seen spraying during a test flight. Note that the flight deck emergency doors have been removed, just in case.

The Mi-6PZh-2 prototype in rather weathered condition at the Central Russian Air Force Museum in Monino.

Mi-6A CCCP-69316 makes a demonstration flight at Le Bourget.

front were stowed under the fuselage, swinging down by means of cables and pulleys for replenishing the water supply in the hover. Alternatively, the helicopter could carry six externally slung bag-type tanks, each holding 1.5 tons (3,310 lb) of fire retardant, in a special net. The Mi-6PZh prototype was converted from the abovementioned commercial demonstrator (CCCP-06174), receiving an appropriate red/white colour scheme. After a series of test flights, the helicopter was exhibited at the 27th Paris Air Show in June 1967. Right after the show the Mi-6PZh was called upon to fight a forest fire near Marseilles in southern France; tragically, on 6th August 1967 it crashed near Le Rove during a fire-fighting sortie, killing the Soviet-French crew captained by Mil' OKB test pilot Yuriy A. Garnayev.

A more refined fire-fighting variant was built in 1971. Designated **Mi-6PZh-2**, it differed from its predecessor in having a water cannon on a flexible mount under the nose.

The helicopter successfully passed state acceptance tests and was used operationally on numerous occasions. Several Mi-6s were converted to this standard; one of them, coded '41 Yellow' (c/n 9683901V), is on display at the Central Russian Air Force Museum in Monino.

Gradually, enough design improvements were accumulated over the first ten years to result in a new baseline version of the helicopter – the **Mi-6A**, which was brought out in 1971. It differed from the original Mi-6 *sans suffixe* mainly in having a higher maximum AUW of 44 tons (97,020 lb), new avionics and modified hydraulic system with an integrated hydraulic unit. Furthermore,

A Russian Air Force Mi-6A coded '52 Red' in a winter setting. Note the second rectangular sliding window at the radio operator's station; the APU on the port cargo door had been added on late Mi-6s *sans suffixe.*

The open clamshell cargo doors and loading ramps of a Mi-6A; the absence of the large cutouts characteristic of the Mi-6 *sans suffixe* is clear to see.

the service life of the main subassemblies was increased. The Mi-6A could transport 90 troops and the maximum slung load rose to 9 tons (19,845 lb). The Mi-6A was produced in both military and civil versions, the latter lacking the NUV machine-gun mount under the nose and having other detail differences. From 1972 onwards military Mi-6As were fitted as standard with an inert gas pressurisation system protecting the fuel tanks against explosions if hit by enemy fire.

An SAR version of the Mi-6A equivalent to the Mi-6PS prototype was brought out as the **Mi-6APS** (called **Mi-6PSA** in some sources). A small number of helicopters were converted to Mi-6APS standard by aircraft repair plants, entering service with the Soviet Air Force; such machines were identifiable by the 'lightning bolt' running the full length of the fuselage.

A **communications relay version** of the Mi-6 was created in 1974 by installing a potent set of radio communications equipment in the cargo cabin, supplemented by additional aerials on the fuselage sides and on the tailboom. It was not built in series.

The **Mi-6VKP** (*vozdooshnyy komahndnyy poonkt* – airborne command post) was evolved from the production Mi-6 by the 535th ARZ. In reality this 'airborne command post' belied its name, since it could only perform its functions after landing and deploying its equipment on the ground. The work started in late 1972 under the guidance of Major D. M. Mel'nikov. The Mi-6VKP was intended for controlling the troops of a ground forces army or an air army. The cargo cabin housed a secure communications suite and a 'war room' for headquarters officers. The Konotop plant converted a total of 36 Rostov-built Mi-6As to Mi-6VKP standard. This version was readily identifiable by the three large blade aerials on the tailboom immediately ahead of the stabilisers, the large 'towel rail' aerial under the tailboom and the vertical rod aerials mounted on brackets on the centre fuselage sides in line with the engine exhausts. Two telescopic aerials were carried on the main gear units, to be removed and erected with bracing wires outside the helicopter after landing.

Somewhat later the Mil' OKB developed its own ABCP version of the Mi-6A – a true airborne command post capable of performing its functions in flight as well as on the ground. The machine bore the manufacturer's designation **Mi-6AYa** – that is, Mi-6A modified under the *Yakhont* (Sapphire) programme, albeit the military chose to call it **Mi-6VzPU** (*vozdooshnyy poonkt oopravleniya* – ABCP) or **Mi-22**. Outwardly it differed from the Mi-6VKP in having one large blade aerial above the root of the tailboom and a string of smaller blade aerials along the fuselage underside; the telescopic aerials were still carried on the main gear units to permit ground deployment. Also, the AI-8 APU on the port side was replaced by a more powerful Stoopino Machinery Design Bureau TA-6 APU on the starboard side. This version was built in series and entered squadron service in 1975.

The designation **Mi-6TZ** (**top**livoza-**prav**shchik – refuelling tanker) was allocated to versions intended to provide refuelling facilities to Army and Air Force units. Such a version was envisaged at an early project stage but did not materialise until the late 1960s. The first variety to enter service was the **Mi-6TZ-SV** (the SV stands for sookho**put**nyye voys**ka** – ground forces), but in fact these machines were used for refuelling Tactical Aviation aircraft and Army Aviation helicopters on the ground. The cargo cabin housed two extra tanks with a total capacity of 7,400 litres (1,628 Imp gal), an NS-30 pump unit, two drums with hoses and nozzles and other necessary equipment. Special canisters were provided for lubricants and alcohol. Generally speaking, any production Mi-6 could be converted into such a tanker.

In 1966 the Mi-6 ceded its title of the most powerful helicopter to the Mil' V-12 *Homer* twin-rotor helicopter. It deserves mention that in 1959 the Mi-6 became the basis for the Mi-10 *Harke* heavy-lift helicopter optimised for carrying outsize loads; however, this type lies outside the scope of this book.

'12 Red', a Russian Air Force Mi-22 airborne command post (c/n 0699V), shows off the single large blade aerial on top of the tailboom and the array of smaller ventral blade aerials.

# Experiments and Projects

In the first half of the 1960s military test pilots conducted experiments with in-flight refuelling of the Mi-4 helicopter, using the Mi-6 as a tanker, but this work did not proceed further than the experimental stage.

The **Mi-6M** designation was reused in 1967 when on 26th November the Council of Ministers issued a directive tasking the OKB with developing a helicopter capable of transporting 11-20 tons (22,255-44,100 lb) of cargo over a distance of 800-1,200 km (496-745 miles). In this case the M suffix denoted *modifitseerovannyy* (modified); the helicopter had a retractable undercarriage and a new main rotor head, among other things. However, more profound studies revealed that the scope for increasing the helicopter's payload would be very limited if the five-blade main rotor were to be retained. Hence development of the Mi-6M was discontinued in 1970 and the OKB embarked on the development of a third-generation heavy helicopter which eventually became the Mi-26.

In 1969 a Mi-6 was converted into a **flying testbed for the D-25VF engine** (F = *forseerovannyy* – uprated) with a take-off rating of 6,500 eshp; this engine had been developed for the Mil' V-12 heavy-lift helicopter. The testbed was also used for studying ways and means of improving the performance of the basic Mi-6. One more Mi-6 ('88 Red', c/n 8683904V) was converted in 1975 within the Mi-26 development programme, becoming an **aerodynamics testbed** fitted with the main and tail rotors of the new machine; it also served for testing the a number of other systems and units of the Mi-26.

The year of 1976 saw the development of the **Mi-6VR** water-spraying testbed (aptly dubbed *Vodoley*, Aquarius) which served for testing the de-icing systems of other helicopters. The cargo cabin housed a water tank and the water was fed to ventral spraybars installed immediately ahead of the cargo door threshold to create icing conditions; the spraybars were forward-swept and were braced to the wing undersurface by long struts.

An artist's impression of the second helicopter to be designated Mi-6M – an early precursor of the Mi-26. Note the retractable landing gear and the faired main rotor head.

Mi-6 '88 Red' (c/n 8683904V), an aerodynamics testbed for the eight-blade main rotor of the Mi-26, at the Mil' OKB's flight test facility in Panki in 1975, with the second prototype V-12 in the background.

THE Mi-6 IN ACTION

# The Mi-6 in Action

**I**n the USSR, most of the Mi-6s were delivered to the Armed Forces where the process of forming independent helicopter regiments reporting directly to the headquarters of various mechanised infantry or tank armies started in the early 1960s. With the advent of the Mi-6 these units came to have a mixed inventory: two squadrons flying Mi-6s (each with 12-15 machines) and two squadrons equipped with Mi-4s, and later Mi-8 *Hip* medium helicopters. As the Mi-6's production rate built up, one such regiment was included into each Military District (MD) and each group of Soviet forces stationed abroad. For example, the Group of Soviet Forces in Germany (GSFG; renamed Western Group of Forces in 1989) included the 239th OGVP (*otdel'nyy Gvardeyskiy vertolyotnyy polk* – Independent Guards Helicopter Regiment) based at Brandis AB; other Mi-6 units were the 340th OVP at Kalinov (L'vov Region) in the Carpathian MD, the 51st OGVP at Aleksandriya AB (Kirovograd Region) in the Kiev MD, the 320th OVP at Kherson (Crimea Region) in the Red Banner Odessa MD, the 280th OVP at Kagan (Turkmenistan) in the Central Asian MD and the 181st OVP at Dzhambul (now Zhambyl, southern Kazakhstan) in the Turkestan MD. There is an interesting aspect of the organisation of the helicopter regiments: attempts were repeatedly made to transfer these units from the Air Force to the Army Aviation (after all, they had been set up precisely to cater for the interests of the ground forces). However, it was not until late 1991 that this organisational structure took its final shape.

The Mi-6 also entered service with independent squadrons and composite air regiments which supported the functioning of headquarters of the many Defence Districts, Groups of Forces and Air Armies. Such units operated a mixed bag of transport and special-purpose aircraft and helicopters. As a rule, their complement included one or two Mi-6VKPs or Mi-22s, sometimes supplemented by an equal number of ordinary transport *Hooks*. For example, the 456th GvOSAP (*Gvardeyskiy otdel'nyy smeshannyy aviapolk* – Independent Guards Composite Air Regiment) at Gavryshevka AB near Vinnitsa, the Ukraine, had a Mi-22; the GSFG's 296th OVE (*otdel'naya vertolyotnaya eskadril'ya* – Independent Helicopter Squadron) at Mahlwinkel AB had two Mi-6VKPs at its disposal. The big Mil' machines were also operated by SAR units stationed in the areas where Soviet recoverable spacecraft returned to Earth: an air detachment in Aral'sk (Kyzyl-Orda Region, Kazakhstan); squadrons in Cheben'ki (Orenburg Region, Russia) and in Karaganda (Kazakhstan), a regiment in Troitsk (Kustanai Region, Kazakhstan).

Initially Air Force crews mastered the Mi-6 with assistance from factory crews. Later, conversion training was conducted in a special centre at Lugansk, the Ukraine, and a regiment stationed at Torzhok (Kalinin Region, Russia) led the way for the service introduction of the Mi-6. The latter regiment subsequently became the core of the Army Aviation's 344th TsBP i PLS (*Tsentr boyevoy podgotovki i pereoochivaniya lyotnovo sostahva* – Combat Training & Aircrew Conversion Centre). When the Mi-6 became operational, helicopter pilots finally entered the gas turbine era as the last among military airmen to do so. The machine's capabil-

A Mi-6 *sans suffixe* supports an assault operation during a Soviet Armed Forces exercise, with a BTR-152 armoured personnel carrier in the foreground.

**Above:** An ASU-76 light SP gun with the Soviet Airborne Troops badge is unloaded by a Mi-6, one of several participating in a landing assault during an exercise.

**Below:** Five early-production Mi-6s with tapered main rotor blades rest between sorties at a forward operating location.

**Opposite page, top:** Soviet Army soldiers prepare to board a Mi-6 *sans suffixe* during an exercise.

ities caused admiration on the part of the aircrews, and this served as an additional incentive for those mastering the helicopter.

The Mi-6 proved to be very stable and easy to fly in cruise mode. However, at low speeds considerable vibrations set in; besides, when flying with a high all-up weight – that is, in excess of 42,500 kg (93,700 lb) – the Mi-6 was clearly underpowered. Hence rolling take-offs and roll-on landings soon became standard operational procedure for the type; this made it possible not only to increase the take-off weight but also to overcome the vibrations more quickly. The new helicopter differed appreciably from the Mi-4 in its piloting techniques; in particular, it was much more sluggish. While in its performance the Mi-6 was superior to any other helicopter of the day, on many other counts the initial-production machines could scarcely lay claim to being new-generation rotorcraft. The service life before the first overhaul was initially 300 hours, later increasing to 600 hours. The AP-31V autopilot and the main hydraulic system gave rise to many complaints; the helicopter had no APU, and starting the engines drained the DC batteries quickly. Nearly all early-production Mi-6s up to and including the 20th Rostov-built batch were sent to the 535th ARZ in Konotop. Here they were not merely refurbished – they were

endowed with new qualities that made them easier to operate. Here are a few examples. It was in Konotop that the early-production Mi-6s were retrofitted with the AI-8 APU and the MSRP-12 FDR; a complete replacement of the electric circuitry was also made. Later the 12th ARZ in Khabarovsk started overhauling the Mi-6s operated east of the Urals.

Early-production D-25V engines were extremely troublesome. For one thing, they were prone to surging. Even more dangerous, however, was their propensity for overspeeding of the free turbine which often ended in uncontained failure. This process developed very swiftly; as the turbine disintegrated, the red-hot fragments flew in all directions with a savage force, destroying everything in their path. The majority of such uncontained failures occurred in flight and ended in crashes. Eventually, to cure the problem the Mi-6 was fitted with a free turbine protection system which automatically shut the engine down, should the free turbine's RPM exceed the red line.

The improvements introduced on the Mi-6 and the Mi-6A over the years usually incurred a weight penalty, yet they achieved their purpose. The helicopter became a reliable combat machine well liked by its crews and capable of fulfilling its missions successfully. The most important mission was probably the delivery of nuclear warheads

from depots to ballistic missile launch sites and airbases where missile strike aircraft were deployed. Such missions were shrouded in utmost secrecy, and each helicopter regiment flying Mi-6s had several hand-picked crews which had an appropriate security clearance. Furthermore, the service introduction of the Mi-6 held the promise of endowing the ground forces with a hitherto unseen level of mobility.

The first combat operation involving Soviet Air Force Mi-6s was probably the invasion of the Warsaw Pact forces into rebellious Czechoslovakia. During the night of 21st August 1968, several Mi-4s and Mi-6s from a helicopter regiment of the Northern Group of Forces stationed in Poland took off from their base at Legnica, landing at Prague's Ruzyne airport; they delivered the first wave of the airborne assault. A helicopter regiment from the Southern Group of Forces also took part in the invasion, leaving its base at Kalocsa, Hungary, to take up temporary residence at Bratislava. Both units stayed in Czechoslovakia for more than a year. During this period the Mi-6s were used very actively for airlifting materiel (including armoured personnel carriers), ammunition and foodstuffs.

Already during the first weeks after the invasion cases were recorded when Soviet Mi-4s came under heavy machine-gun fire from the rebels, which led to the loss of at least two machines. In consequence, the Mi-6s started flying at an altitude of 4,000 m (13,100 ft) to stay out of range of the HMGs. Climb to this altitude and descent from it was performed in a steep spiral in the airfield area.

Much the same techniques were used during the Afghan War (1979-89) which marked the culmination of the Mi-6's combat career in the Soviet Armed Forces. The 280th OVP from Kagan AB (Central Asian MD) with two squadrons of Mi-6s was the first to deploy, taking up residence in Kandahar on 2nd January 1980. During the same year the 181st OVP with two squadrons of Mi-6s redeployed to Kunduz, which was also home for a further Mi-6 squadron staffed with Soviet specialists and operating in support of the government troops of the Democratic Republic of Afghanistan. Additionally, pairs of Mi-6s were on detachment at Kabul and Shindand. To cater for the needs of the relatively small 40th Army (the Soviet contingent in Afghanistan), it proved necessary to build up a very large helicopter task force which included as many as 60 Mi-6s by the mid-1980s.

The helicopters made an excellent showing during operations in the mountains, displaying their ability to maintain confidently an altitude in excess of 6,000 m (19,690 ft) which was unattainable for the smaller Mi-8s. Their agility was also quite adequate, enabling them to operate into short mountain airstrips. The main missions flown by the Mi-6s in Afghanistan were supply flights. The helicopters carried artillery pieces, vehicles, ammunition and, most notably, food;

the 181st OVP at Kunduz even had a 'Meat Express Special' Mi-6 with a refrigerated cabin. Transportation of slung loads was performed in exceptional cases, mainly for the purpose of salvaging downed helicopters of other types. In the summer (in 'hot and high' conditions) the Mi-6 could lug 4-4.5 tons (8,820-9,920 lb) of cargo in a single sortie – two to three times as much as the Mi-8 in the same conditions; in the winter this rose to 6-7 tons (13,230-15,430 lb). Casualty evacuation (codenamed *grooz **trista**, 'cargo 300') was another important role – and, sadly but inevitably, so was the

**Above:** Troops disembark Mi-6 *sans suffixe* c/n 1030803V after landing. Note how the star insignia were carried on the wings.

**Below:** '06 Red', a very late Mi-6 *sans suffixe* (c/n 705302V), airlifts a UTI-MiG-15 as a slung load. Note the 'Excellent aircraft' maintenance award badge aft of the flight deck.

Not all Soviet military Mi-6s were Air Force aircraft. This helicopter coded '47 Yellow' is a Soviet Navy/North Fleet machine.

retrieval of Soviet servicemen killed in action for burial at home (known as *grooz **dve**sti*, 'cargo 200').

Only very rarely did the Mi-6s participate in landing assault operations in Afghanistan – above all, due to the risk of high personnel losses in the event of a shootdown; when they did, they came in on the second wave, when the landing zone had been secured. One such landing operation in 1982 resulted in a scandal when the assault helicopters bound for Rabat-e-Jali crossed the border because of a navigation error and landed the assault party in Iran.

Inevitably, there were combat losses. The first loss of a Mi-6 in Afghanistan was in 1981, when a helicopter landed on a dirt strip at Lashkargakh which, unbeknownst to the crew, had been mined by the Mujahideen rebels. There were no fatalities on that occasion; other Mi-6 crews were not so lucky. On 17th September 1985 a Mi-6 carrying twenty 200-litre (55-gal) fuel drums exploded in mid-air after taking multiple hits; only the co-pilot survived. Incidentally, 1985 was the year when Mi-6 losses in the war peaked at seven, including one machine lost in a ground collision with an Afghan Air Force Sukhoi Su-22 *Fitter* fighter-bomber.

The Mi-6 showed fairly high resistance to small arms fire, but nevertheless urgent measures were taken to enhance its survivability, especially since the Mujahideen had Stinger and Redeye anti-aircraft missiles. The fuel tanks were filled with explosion suppression polyurethane foam, and ASO-2V infrared countermeasures flare dispensers were added. Exhaust/air mixers reducing the heat signature were also tried but did not find wide use.

It has to be said that Soviet Air Force Mi-6s had their share of peacetime accident attrition. For example, on 11th December 1990 Mi-6 *sans suffixe* c/n 1030903V captained by Capt. Mikhail I. Vitushenko crashed near Kobrin, Belorussia, during a messed-up landing approach in fog when the pilots lost attitude awareness; only one of the six crewmembers survived.

A notable chapter in the biography of the Soviet Air Force's Mi-6s was their employment in the national economy; they were used alongside Aeroflot aircraft for delivering civilian cargoes to remote corners of the Soviet Union in case of need. These helicopters were also engaged in SAR operations to locate and recover the re-entry modules of Soviet manned and automatic space vehi-

The Mi-6 was much used operationally during the Afghan War. These two helicopters are seen at Pul-e-Khumri in Afghanistan in January 1987.

cles. Along with special aviation units assigned to the Cosmonaut Detachment, crews from the 181st OVP took an active part in these operations; when this regiment was despatched to Afghanistan, they were replaced by crews from the 157th OVP. The main task of the Mi-6 was to deliver the recoverable module to an airfield from where it was transported further by an An-12 turboprop. The crews fulfilled their missions day and night in any weather.

When the Chernobyl' nuclear meltdown occurred on 26th April 1986, the 51st OGVP at Aleksandriya was sent to the area to participate in the damage control operations. Initially the Mi-6s performed transportation flights; when the disaster relief teams started burying the disabled reactor of the power station's Unit 4, the Mi-6s were used for carrying externally slung loads of sand and lead slabs and dropping them on the demolished reactor building. When the radiation doscs accumulated by the crews reached 25 Roentgen, the Ministry of Defence started sending crews from all over the Soviet Union to Chernobyl' to relieve the crews from Aleksandriya. After the completion of the work at least nine Mi-6s, which defied decontamination, had to be struck off charge and relegated to the radioactive hardware storage and disposal depot at Booryakovka (aka Rassokha).

Export deliveries of the Mi-6 started in 1964; up to the 1980s; more than 60 of these helicopters were purchased by 13 nations. The first foreign customer was Indonesia; nine Mi-6s were delivered to an Indonesian Air Force unit at Atang Sanjaya AB near Bogor, West Java Province, in 1964. However, their career proved to be brief: just four years later the helicopters were retired. In the 1960s a small number of Mi-6s were delivered to what was then North Vietnam, providing a much-needed heavy-lift capability. The Mi-6s were operated by the North Vietnamese Air Force's 916th Helicopter Regiment 'Bà Vi' (Three Summits) of the 371st Air Division at Hoa Lac AB not far from Hanoi. Further Asian operators of the type

were China (the 1st Army Aviation Regiment at Jinan received a small number of Mi-6s in the 1970s) and Laos (two examples were delivered to the Lao People's Liberation Army Air Force by 1988). A little-known fact is that the Pakistan Army Aviation Corps purchased a single Mi-6 for evaluation purposes. The results were disappointing and the Pakistanis scrapped the helicopter without ever putting it into service.

In the Middle East the Mi-6 was first delivered to the United Arab Republic, which received an initial batch of 12 helicopters before June 1967. Later, when the UAR split up, further deliveries were made to the air arms of its former constituent parts – Egypt, which received enough to equip a squadron by October 1973, and Syria, which had more than ten Mi-6s. One of the Egyptian Mi-6s was sold to the USA for evaluation in the 1970s. The Iraqi Air Force was one more customer for the type, receiving 14 by September 1980. In Africa the type saw service with the air arms of Algeria (four of these helicopters were delivered, originally wearing quasi-civil registrations in the 7T-W** series), Angola (where they served with the 21st Transport Helicopter Regiment/1st Helicopter Squadron) and Ethiopia, which had ten such helicopters on strength with one squadron. In South America the Mi-6 saw service with the Peruvian Air Force.

As for the Soviet Union's closest (both geographically and politically) allies – the Warsaw Pact nations, Poland was the only customer. Three civil-registered Mi-6As were delivered to the Instalbud agency (*Instalacja i budowa* – Installation & Construction) in 1975-79 for use as 'flying cranes'. In 1986 they were transferred to the Polish Air Force, which operated them until July 1990; two of the three helicopters were then sold to the Ukraine.

Conversion training of flight and ground crews from the countries which had acquired the Mi-6 was conducted at the Kremenchug Civil Aviation Flying School. The Mi-6s delivered to foreign customers had their designated TBO understated.

Russian Air Force Mi-6 '16 Yellow' (c/n 705305V) in an unusual green/black camouflage scheme at Kubinka AB near Moscow in 1992.

An Egyptian Air Force Mi-6 serialled 885 in an overall desert camouflage scheme.

Two Indonesian Air Force Mi-6s, with H-275 nearest to the camera.

The combat career of the Mi-6 abroad started in 1967 during the conflicts in Indo-China and in the Middle East. Its participation in the third Arab-Israeli war, aka Six-Day War (5th-11th June 1967), was more than deplorable: ten of the 12 Mi-6s in the UAR Air Force inventory were destroyed on the ground at their bases (Bir Thamada and Bir Gifgafa) by Israeli air strikes on the opening day of the hostilities. After the war, the Soviet Union supplied more Mi-6s as attrition replacements, and by the time the fourth Arab-Israeli war, aka Yom Kippur War, broke out in October 1973 the Egyptian Air Force had a combat-ready squadron of these helicopters. As distinct from the EAF's Mi-8s, the Mi-6s did not operate over the battlefield and in the enemy's immediate rear during the Yom Kippur War, being considered too vulnerable; they were used mainly for airlifting various loads in the interests of the units of the second echelon.

Conversely, during the Vietnam War the type displayed its best qualities to advantage. Initially the Mi-6s of the North Vietnamese Air Force's 919th Regiment operated within the territory of North Vietnam, transporting cargoes, small army units and repair teams engaged in the restoration of bridges and road stretches destroyed by US bombardments. At first, as noted by various sources, the heavy helicopters were flown by Aeroflot crews; later the new hardware was fully mastered by local airmen. The Mi-6 played a very useful role in the so-called programme for enhancing the survivability of

Polish Air Force Mi-6A '063 White'.

the NVAF's fighter element. The Mi-6 helicopters airlifted MiG-17 or MiG-21 fighters to splendidly camouflaged tactical airstrips or to shelters in the mountains at a distance of 10-30 km (6.2-18.6 miles) from the main airfields, or even to the territory of neutral China where they were safe from US air strikes. When the air raids were over, the fighters returned to their bases, resuming combat sorties. For example, in November 1967, shortly before a USAF raid on Noi Bai AB, the Vietnamese (which had been alerted in a timely fashion) succeeded in evacuating the fighters. Apart from aircraft, surface-to-air missile (SAM) systems were also redeployed over short distances. The Mi-6s also performed airlift missions in the interests of the troops on the offensive; they took part in the Vietnamese Army's blitzkrieg against the Khmer Rouge in Kampuchea in 1979.

The Mi-6 enhanced its good reputation in the course of the Ethiopian-Somali War in Ogaden Province in July 1977 – March 1978. The Ethiopian Air Force's Mi-6s carried out a large scope of work during the preparation and execution of a counteroffensive. Another African country where the type was at war is Angola, where Angolan People's Air Force Mi-6s were used against the UNITA guerrillas; three of the helicopters were reportedly destroyed in October-November 1985.The *Hook* was used fairly widely by Iraq during the Iran-Iraq War which broke out in September 1980. In the course of the eight-year war the Mi-6s were used both for landing tactical assault groups and for transport missions. Several machines were reported lost due to enemy action, including attacks by Islamic Republic of Iran Air Force Bell AH-1 Huey Cobra combat helicopters. In August 1990 the Mi-6s took part in Saddam Hussein's invasion of Kuwait. There is no reliable information as to how they fared in Operation *Desert Storm* (that is, whether they survived the Allied air strikes).

In post-Soviet days the Mi-6 had a chance to 'smell gunpowder' in several hot spots of the former Soviet Union – so much for the 'fraternity of all peoples' that the nation used to pride itself on. In early March

1992 Russian Air Force Mi-6s took part in evacuating the personnel and materiel of the 366th Mechanised Infantry Regiment from Stepanakert, the capital of the Nagornyy Karabakh enclave that was the apple of discord between Armenia and Azerbaijan. At that time the machines flew some 30 sorties, coming under fire from both belligerents but suffering no losses. Russian Air Force Mi-6s saw action again, albeit on a small scale, in the First Chechen War (1994-96), delivering supplies to Khankala airbase a short way from Groznyy – again without losses to the Chechen separatists.

When the former Soviet military assets were up for grabs, Georgia was among the new proprietors of the Mi-6; judging by the scant information carried by the media, the Georgian machines were occasionally used for transport missions in support of its troops engaged in the civil war in Abkhazia (1992-93). Radical organisational changes took place in the helicopter regiments inherited by the Ukraine, which kept a sizeable number of Mi-6s. In 1992 the 51st OGVP at Aleksandriya was transformed into an Independent Helicopter Brigade of the National Guard. In September 1997 two Ukrainian Army Aviation Mi-6s were used for dropping paratroopers during Exercise *Cossack Steppe* which was conducted at the Shirokiy Lan test range near Nikolayev with the participation of Ukrainian, British and Polish troops.

Immaculate Vietnamese Air Force Mi-6A '7609 Red' preserved in a Hanoi museum.

The Ukraine kept a number of ex-Soviet Mi-6s; camouflaged Mi-6A '65 Red' is shown here in the 1990s.

# Civil Operations

The commercial career of the Mi-6 began almost concurrently with the type's introduction into Soviet Air Force service. The first civil operator was GosNII GVF (*Gosudarstvennyy naoochno-issledovatel'skiy instittoot Grazhdahnskovo vozdooshnovo flota* – the State Civil Air Fleet Research Institute), which received its first Mi-6 in 1961; two years later the Kremenchug Civil Aviation Flying School (Kremenchug, Poltava Region) also received a few Mi-6s and stated training Aeroflot crews. The helicopter's capabilities, which were fantastic by the standards of the day, proved to be a great boon for the national economy: new oil and natural gas deposits were being actively explored then, primarily in Siberia and in the North where the transport network was virtually non-existent.

In Soviet times the Mi-6 saw service with at least 15 of Aeroflot's United Air Detachments in 11 Civil Aviation Directorates – mostly based east of the Urals and in the North. These were the Northern CAD/ 2nd Arkhangel'sk UAD/68th Flight at Arkhangel'sk-Vas'kovo (it was transferred to the Arkhangel'sk CAD in 1971 when the Northern CAD was dissolved); the Far Eastern CAD/2nd Khabarovsk UAD/249th Flight at Khabarovsk-MVL; the Komi CAD's Pechora UAD/338th Flight and Ukhta UAD/302nd Flight; the Krasnoyarsk CAD's 2nd Krasnoyarsk UAD and Noril'sk UAD/329th Flight at Noril'sk-Alykel'; the Magadan CAD/Chaunskoye UAD/151st Flight; the Moscow Agricultural Work & Commuter Air Traffic Directorate (later Central Regions CAD)/Myachkovo UAD at Moscow-Myachkovo; the Turkmen CAD/Ashkhabad UAD/166th Flight; the Tyumen' CAD's 1st Tyumen' UAD/438th Flight, Nizhnevartovsk UAD/441st Flight, Salekhard UAD/388th Flight and Surgut UAD/121st Flight (the latter unit was initially in the Urals CAD); and the Yakutian CAD/Nyurba UAD/270th Flight.

As early as 1963-64 the airmen of the Tyumen' CAD logged about 600 hours and transported nearly 3,500 tons (7,875,000 lb) of cargoes. It should be noted that the mastering of the new helicopter by Aeroflot proceeded at a quicker pace as compared to the

Aeroflot Mi-6s were much used during construction work in outback areas; here, CCCP-11286 carries a high-voltage power line pylon.

Civil Mi-6As served on until 2002. Resplendent in orange/blue basic Aeroflot colours for helicopters flying in Polar regions, Mi-6A RA-21067 was operated by UTair.

Air Force. This was due to the greater experience characteristic of Aeroflot pilots who logged considerably more flight hours per year than their military colleagues.

Crews from nearly all Aeroflot detachments operating the type worked in the regions where oil and natural gas prospecting and other major industrial projects were taking place; for instance, Mi-6s belonging to the Turkmen CAD saw a lot of action in the oil-rich Tyumen' Region. This made it possible, for example, to concentrate up to 40-50 Mi-6s in the north of the Tyumen' Region; it will not be an exaggeration to say that without their participation the USSR would have received oil from that region much later. In 1963-65, Mi-6s were used for trial transportation of large-diameter steel pipes during the construction of the Shaim-Tyumen' and Igrim-Urals oil pipelines; each pipe was more than 30 m (100 ft) long and weighed nearly 7 tons (15,430 lb). The Mi-6 was heavily involved in the construction of every single major oil or gas pipeline built in the ensuing decades. The use of helicopters made it possible to achieve an appreciably higher tempo of the on-site preparations and commission the pipelines on schedule.

Civil crews flew the Mi-6 with slung loads much more often than military crews. This was due not so much to the large number of outsize cargoes, but rather to the low efficiency of the Mi-6 when transporting cargoes internally. The onboard cargo handling devices were limited to a winch which permitted only hauling the pipes into the cabin through the rear loading hatch; for this reason the winch was used very rarely. Therefore it took much time and arduous work to fill the spacious cabin.

The younger Mi-6As stayed in service long enough to see the demise of the Soviet Union and the disintegration of the all-Union Aeroflot into numerous airlines. Post-Soviet commercial operators of the type included Komiavia (later Komiaviatrans), Tyumen'AviaTrans (later rebranded UTair)

and Turkmenistan Airlines/Akhal Aircompany.

Unfortunately the Mi-6's civil operations were not without accidents either – for various reasons. Sometimes Mother Nature was to blame; for instance, on 12th June 1976 Mi-6 *sans suffixe* CCCP-21875 of the Komi CAD/Ukhta UAD/302nd Flight came down in a forest 19 km (11.8 miles) from Kedva settlement, Ukhta Region, after losing control in severe turbulence. On other occasions the tell-tale human factor was the cause. On 26th August 1974 Mi-6A CCCP-21157 (c/n 737110V – that is, year of manufacture 1973, Batch 71, 10th helicopter in the batch) of the Arkhangel'sk CAD/2nd Arkhangel'sk UFD/68th Flight crashed 110 km (68.35 miles) south-east of Vorkuta, hitting a hillside after deviating from the designated air route below minimum safe altitude. In another case of human error, Mi-6A CCCP-21019 (c/n 0539, meaning unknown) belonging to the abovementioned 302nd Flight was totalled after force-landing in autorotation mode near Kharasavey airport on 12th July 1986 when both engines flamed out because the fuel system was operated incorrectly.

Sometimes, however, the cause was hardware failure; no doubt, this was due partly to the wear and tear the helicopters were subjected to. It was such an accident that eventually caused the type to be retired altogether. On 21st July 2002 Mi-6A RA-21074 operated by Noril'sk Avia went missing en route from Noril'sk to Cape Chelyuskin with a team of prospectors. The wreckage was not discovered until several days later; there were no survivors among the nine crew and 12 passengers. The 'tin kickers' quickly established that the main gearbox had disintegrated in flight, causing a massive fire. After that, the CIS Interstate Aviation Committee cancelled the Mi-6's type certificate. At present the Mi-6 has been superseded in both military and civil applications by the Mi-26.

# The Mi-6A in Detail

The Mi-6A is a military and commercial multi-purpose helicopter designed for day/night operation in visual meteorological conditions (VMC). It has a crew of five. The airframe is of riveted all-metal construction and is mostly made of D16T duralumin and V95T aluminium alloy; additionally, AK-6 and AL-9 aluminium alloys, ML5, VM65-1 and MA-8 magnesium alloys, VT1-1 titanium alloy and 30KhGSA, 18KhNMA, 1Kh18N9T, 40KhNMA, OKhN3MFA, 45, 25 and 20 grade steel are used.

The semi-monocoque fuselage of basically oval cross-section has frames, longerons and stringers; the skin thickness varies from 0.8 to 2.5 mm (0½₂ in to 0³⁄₃₂ in). The fuselage consists of four sections, each with its own numbering of frames. The *forward fuselage* has 12 frames (Nos. 1-12) and 141 stringers (Nos. 0 and 1R/1L through 70R/70L). It houses the crew section, the avionics and most of the auxiliary equipment. Its cross-section changes from circular at the front to quasi-oval with flattened sides and top. The forward extremity of the stepped nose houses an extensively glazed navigator's station (frames 1-6) with an aft-opening jettisonable entry door to starboard (Frames 2-4). The glazing is made of Perspex 3 mm (0⁷⁄₆₄ in) thick, except for the forward panel, which is made of boron-silicate triplex glass. On military versions the underside of the extreme nose features clamshell doors (frames 1-3) for maintenance access to the NUV-1M machine-gun installation.

The rest of the crew is seated in a spacious flight deck (frames 6-12), the captain on the left and the co-pilot on the right, the flight engineer on the left and the radio operator on the right behind them. The glazing features four optically flat windshield panes (the inner two are 4-mm (0⁵⁄₃₂ in) Perspex and the outer two triplex glass), two eyebrow windows and four side windows. The first pair of side windows are sliding direct vision windows bulged for better downward visibility and are built into jettisonable emergency escape doors for the pilots (frames 5-8); there is also a jettisonable emergency escape door to port (frames 9-12) for the rest of the crew. The flight deck roof incorporates a forward-hinged hatch (frames 8-9) opening outwards for access to the engines and main rotor head on the ground; steps are fitted above the rear side windows to permit safe access. Two battery compartments are located low on the port side of the forward fuselage. The forward fuselage terminates in a bulkhead with a door giving access to the freight hold.

The *centre fuselage* has 42 frames; Nos. 1, 5, 8, 10, 14, 18, 22, 26, 31, 38 and 42 are mainframes absorbing the principal loads. The troop/cargo cabin with a stressed floor 11.725 m (38 ft 5⅝ in) long is located between frames 1-26; it has a maximum width of 2.72 mm (8 ft 11 in) and a maximum height of 2.595 m (8 ft 6⅛ in). The cabin floor rests on the lower portions of frames 1-26 and two longerons; it incorporates a hatch for the external sling system (frames 14-18) which is closed by two pairs of doors. Bays for eight fuel tanks are located under the floor between frames 2 and 22.

At the aft of the cabin end is a cargo hatch measuring 2.65 x 2.7 m (8 ft 8¹¹⁄₃₂ in x 8 ft 2²⁷⁄₆₄ in) closed by hydraulically actuated clamshell doors. Their lower forward portions are cut away to avoid encroaching on the cabin width when open; the resulting aperture is closed by a triangular flap hinged to the cargo hatch sill. The port clamshell door carries the APU. Three detachable vehicle loading ramps can be hooked up to the sill to create a full-width ramp. Personnel access to the interior is via three outward-opening aft-hinged rectangular doors – two to port and one to starboard (frames 8-10 and 22-24); these are regarded as emergency exits. As standard there are nine circular cabin windows to port and ten to starboard; the Perspex glazing is 3 mm thick. Two of the windows open, permitting air hoses from an air heater to be inserted for pre-heating the engines and the main gearbox in the winter.

Positioned above the cabin are the engine bay (frames 1-14) and the main gearbox bay (frames 14-18), aft of which are three more fuel tank bays (one between frames 19-22 and two side by side between frames 22-26). Detachable panels protecting piping and cable runs from damage are fitted to the cabin walls and ceiling.

The *tailboom* is a tapered stressed-skin structure with 18 frames and 28 stringers; the skin thickness is 1.2 and 1.5 mm (0⁴⁄₆₄ in and 0¹⁄₁₆ in). The tailboom is joined to the centre fuselage by bolts; its diameter is 1.76 m (5 ft 9¹⁹⁄₆₄ in) at the front and 1.2 m (3 ft 11¼ in) at the rear. The tailboom houses the tail rotor transmission shaft, control cables, stabiliser attachment fittings and some avionics and equipment items. The *tail rotor pylon (fin)* featuring 14 ribs is built integrally with a circular-section structure with seven frames mating with the tailboom; its axis is 'kinked' 45°40' upwards relative to the tailboom axis. The tail rotor pylon houses the intermediate gearbox, the final drive gearbox (at rib 14) and a transmission shaft with a support at rib 8. The fixed rudder has an asymmetrical airfoil which serves to off-load the tail rotor as the forward speed increases. It is of riveted construction; the skin is metal on the starboard side (where the tail rotor is) and AM-100 linen fabric on the port side.

The cantilever shoulder-mounted *wings* of trapezoidal planform have no sweepback and no dihedral; incidence 14°15' (port wing) and 15°45' (starboard wing). The wings utilise a TsAGI P35 high-speed airfoil; thickness/chord ratio 15% at root and 12% at tip. The wings are of riveted construction and comprise a centre section beam mounted in attachment fittings between frames 18-19 and two detachable wing panels. The latter comprise a torsion-box type spar, ribs (Nos. 5-32 on each side), stringers, leading-edge and trailing-edge sections and a rounded tip fairing; the wing/fuselage joint is closed by fairings. The skin is made of duralumin 0.6 to 4 mm (approx 0½₂ to 0⁵⁄₃₂ in) thick; air-cooled heat shields made of 0.8-mm (0½₂ in) stainless steel arc located between ribs 8-14 to protect the skin from the hot engine exhaust.

The all-movable *stabilisers* of trapezoidal planform attached to the tailboom provide longitudinal trim in forward flight. Each stabiliser features a spar, nine ribs, a trailing-edge stringer and a rounded tip fairing; the skin is metal ahead of the spar and fabric aft of it. Stabiliser incidence is +5° to −13°, adjusted by a worm-and-roller control mechanism, depending on the collective pitch setting.

The fixed tricycle landing gear has oleo-nitrogen shock absorption. The castoring nose unit attached to centre fuselage frame 1 has twin 720 x 310 mm (28.35 x 12.2 in) K3-27/2 non-braking wheels mounted on a common axle The main units are of three-strut pyramid type; they are attached to centre fuselage frames 18 and 22, mounting 1,325 x 480 mm (52.2 x 18.9 in) KT-67 wheels (*koleso tormoznoye* – brake wheel) with low-pressure tyres and pneumatic expander-tube brakes. A non-retractable tail bumper is provided to protect the tailboom and tail rotor in a tail-down landing. It consists of a shock absorber, two tubular struts and a tailskid made of cast magnesium.

The powerplant consists of two Solov'yov D-25V turboshafts rated at 5,500 shp for take-off and 3,100 shp in cruise mode at 3,100 m (10,170 ft) and 250 km/h (155 mph). The D-25V has a fixed-area intake assembly, a nine-stage axial compressor with bleed valves at the third and fourth stages, a can-annular combustion chamber with 12 flame tubes, a single-stage axial power turbine and a two-stage axial free turbine. Two accessory gearboxes are mounted on the front casing.

Engine pressure ratio (EPR) at take-off power 5.6; power turbine speed at take-off power 10,530 rpm; mass flow at take-off power 26 kg/sec (57 lb/sec); turbine temperature 1,160°K; specific fuel consumption (SFC) 0.287 kg/hp·hr (0.632 lb/hp·hr) at take-off power and 0.343 kg/hp·hr (0.756 lb/hp·hr) at cruise power. Length overall 2,737 mm (8 ft 11¾ in), width 1,086 mm (3 ft 6¾ in), height 1,158 mm (3 ft 9¹⁹⁄₃₂ in), dry

weight 1,243 kg (2,240.8 lb). The designated service life is 6,000 hours.

The engines are installed side by side on top of the centre fuselage between frames 2-14 and attached to the fuselage by adjustable rods connected to six attachment brackets for each engine. The port and starboard engines are interchangeable, except for the handed air-cooled exhaust pipes made of welded Kh18N10T stainless steel.

The D-25V has a recirculation-type pressure lubrication system with an MN-23S primary oil pump, an MNO-23G oil scavenging pump and an MFS-35 oil filter. It comprises two subsystems. The oil system of the engine's power section uses transformer oil or MK-8 grade mineral oil; the free turbine and its power take-off shaft are serviced with a mix-

The flight deck section of an early Mi-6 *sans suffixe* with a convex navigator's station transparency. Note the add-on armour plating.

The nose of a civil Mi-6 with the later-style optically flat navigator's station glazing. Note the doors enclosing the NUV machine-gun mount on military examples.

The engine cowlings and the main rotor head.

ture of MK-22 (or MS-20) oil and transformer oil (or MK-8) – 50/50 in the winter and 75/25 in the summer. The powerplant features a free turbine overspeed protection system and the IV-200G vibration measurement kit.

The engines are started electrically by STG-12GM starter-generators. Engine starting and ground power supply is ensured by an Ivchenko AI-8 APU mounted on the port clamshell door of the cargo hatch, with intake and exhaust orifices.

The engines, together with the main gearbox and the cooling fan assembly, are enclosed by a large fairing incorporating multi-section cowlings. The lower cowling panels on both engines, the cooling fan section and the main gearbox fold down by means of hydraulic rams to act as work platforms during maintenance. The fairing incorporates longitudinal and transverse firewalls made of OT4-0 titanium alloy.

Engine torque is fed via overrunning clutches into the R-7 main gearbox mounted on a truss-type bearer between frames 14-18. It reduces the rotation speed and conveys torque to the main rotor, tail rotor drive shaft and the fan located between the canted sections of the exhaust pipes which serves the engine oil coolers and main gearbox oil cooler. The R-7 is a four-stage gearbox. The first stage has bevel gears and two torque equalising mechanisms, the second stage has four cylindrical gears transmitting torque to a large central gear; the planetary third stage and the fourth stage form a differential mechanism. The overall reduction ratio is 0.01445 for the main rotor drive shaft, 0.2484 for the tail rotor drive shaft and 0.366 for the fan. The main rotor shaft is inclined 5° forward. The freewheeling clutches enable the helicopter to continue flight even if one of the free turbine shafts jams or one of the engines seizes; they also enable the helicopter to land in autorotation mode after a dual engine failure. There are two accessories gearboxes for

the oil pumps, four drives for hydraulic pumps, two drives for AC generators, and two reserve drives. The R-7 also mounts the rotor brake and the autopilot servos. The main gearbox uses a 50/50 mixture of MK-22 (MS-20) and MK-8 or transformer oil in the winter and a 75/25 mixture of the same in the summer. The total amount of oil is approximately 235 litres (51.7 Imp gal).

A drive shaft passing inside the tailboom connects the main gearbox with a V1525-000 intermediate gearbox at the base of the tail rotor pylon turning the axis of the shaft up through 47° and thence with the V1537-000 final drive gearbox which turns the shaft through 90° to starboard. The final drive gearbox incorporates the tail rotor pitch control mechanism.

The five-blade *main rotor* turns clockwise when seen from above. The fully articulated rotor head has axial, flapping and drag hinges with adjustable stops; it is equipped with hydraulic dampers and a 'flapping compensator' which reduces the blades' angle of attack when they start their upward movement. Blade incidence ranges from 1° to 13°30' ±30'. The blade droop angle when at rest is 7°; the maximum flapping angle is 25° ±30'. The main rotor blades have a constant chord of 1,000 mm (39% in) and feature geometrical camber changing in accordance with a linear rule. Each blade has a tubular steel spar and 21 pockets loosely connected with each other; the trailing-edge parts of the pockets feature a metal honeycomb filler. The blade airfoil is NACA 230M up to the 18th pocket, followed by a transitional airfoil and then by a high-speed TsAGI airfoil on pockets 19-21. The blades are provided with balance tabs and a compressed-air spar failure warning system.

The AV-63B four-blade pusher-type *tail rotor* located on the starboard side likewise turns clockwise when seen from the hub. The interchangeable L63-Kh6BP wooden blades of trapezoidal planform are attached to the rotor head by hinges permitting a flapping movement. Blade incidence with the pedals set neutral is 4° ±30', varying from 23°30' ±30' ('hard a-starboard') to –9°30' ±30' ('hard a-port').

The Mi-6 has full dual controls. Pitch and roll control, climb and descent are effected by the swashplate; directional control is effected by changing the tail rotor pitch. The control system is of a mechanical mixed type, with mainly rigid linkages. Cables are used for the tail rotor and stabiliser control at the rear of the centre fuselage, the tailboom and tail rotor pylon. The AP-34B Srs 2 four-channel autopilot ensures the helicopter's stabilisation in yaw, roll, pitch and altitude. Control is effected by RP-28 combined two-chamber servos (*roolevoy privod*) doubling as hydraulic control actuators. An SDV-5000-OA hydraulic damper is installed in the yaw control channel. The system of main rotor collective pitch control incorporates a spring loading device with an ENT-2M electromagnetic brake to warn the pilot that an excessive increase of the collective pitch with the engines at take-off power causes a reduction of the main rotor's RPM. A main rotor speed stabiliser with a KAU-30B actuator (*kombineerovannyy agregaht oopravleniya* – combined control unit) is included into the engine control system.

Internal fuel is carried in 11 bag-type tanks (Nos. 1-8 under the cargo cabin floor and Nos. 9-11 above the cabin). Tank No.1 is a reserve tank; the rest are divided into five groups (Group I, Nos. 2 and 3; Group II, Nos. 4-6; Group III, Nos. 7 and 8; Group IV, Nos. 9 and 10; Group V, No.11). Electric transfer pumps are installed in each group of tanks and the reserve tank, feeding the fuel to the engines' Model 889A delivery pumps, NR-23A fuel control units and TsR-23A centrifugal fuel flow regulators. Two 2,250-litre (495 Imp gal) cylindrical external tanks can be attached to the fuselage sides by locks and N-shaped braces; additionally, two ferry tanks of the same capacity can be installed in the cargo cabin. The internal fuel capacity is 8,250 litres (1,815 Imp gal), increasing to 12,750 litres (2,805 Imp gal) with external tanks and 17,250 litres (3,795 Imp gal) with external tanks and ferry tanks. Fuel usage can be controlled automatically or manually. Fuel grades used are Russian T-1, T-2, TS-1 or TS-1G kerosene, or Western equivalents; grade 'I' anti-gelling agent is added in winter to prevent ice formation. The single-point pressure refuelling connector is located on the starboard side of the forward fuselage.

The fuel tanks are equipped with an inert gas pressurisation system with three 8-litre (1.76 Imp gal) carbon dioxide bottles mounted above the ceiling of the cargo cabin.

Hydraulic power is supplied by NSh-2S gear-type pumps driven off the main gearbox. The *main* and *back-up hydraulic systems* cater for the RP-28 servos and the KAU-30B actuator. When using the main system, two modes of controlling the helicopter are possible: manual control by the pilot and combined control by the pilot with corrections from the autopilot; with the back-up system, only manual control is possible. The *auxiliary hydraulic system* operates the windshield wipers, the doors of the machine-gun mount, the external sling locks, the clamshell cargo doors and vehicle loading ramps, and the engine cowling sections/work platforms. In addition, it unlocks the collective pitch levers and adjusts the pilots' seats in height and seat back angle. All three systems use AMG-10 oil-type hydraulic fluid (*aviatsionnoye mahslo ghidravlicheskoye*); nominal pressure is 120-150 kg/cm² (1,714-2,142 psi). The main and backup systems are fed separately from two 67-litre (14.74 Imp gal) tanks mounted on the GB-1 hydraulic unit (*ghidroblok*); the auxiliary system is fed from the upper section of the back-up system tank.

The pneumatic system actuates the wheel brakes, the engine air bleed control valves, the shutters in the cabin heating air duct and the machine-gun cocking mecha-

The tail rotor and the tail rotor pylon.

The starboard main gear unit of an early Mi-6 (note the airfoil-shaped fairing on the oleo strut).

nism. Compressed air is stored in the upper parts of main gear shock struts doubling as air bottles charged to 50 kg/cm² (714 psi). Replenishment of these bottles with a capacity of 32 litres (7.04 Imp gal) each is effected by an AK-50T compressor mounted on the port engine.

The electric system caters for the avionics, flight and engine instruments, lighting equipment, engine starting, de-icing system and some other items. Primary 27V DC is supplied by two STG-12TM starter-generators, with four 12SAM-55 storage batteries as a back-up. 360V/400 Hz three-phase AC is supplied by two 90-kW SGS-90/360 generators (catering for the main rotor de-icing system), with PT-500Ts (*preobrazovahtel' tryokhfahznyy*) and PAG-1FP three-phase converters and PO-1500 single-phase converters (*preobrazovahtel' odnofahznyy*) supplying AC to the navigation and radio equipment. A ShRAP-500 DC ground power receptacle and a ShRA-200LK AC ground power receptacle are provided on the port side of the centre fuselage. The lighting equipment includes interior lighting, navigation lights on the tailboom and at the wingtips, red anti-collision lights above and below the centre fuselage, formation lights and blade tip lights to avoid collisions during night operations) and ventral floodlights.

The engine air intakes, main rotor blades, flight deck/navigator's station windshields and pitot heads are electrically de-iced. The tail rotor blades are de-iced by a system using an ethyl alcohol/glycerine mixture from a 28-litre (6.16 Imp gal) tank.

Fire protection in the engine bays, main gearbox bay and internal fuel tank bays, as well as inside the engines, is ensured by six OS-8MF fire extinguisher bottles (*ognetooshitel' stationarnyy* – stationary fire extinguisher) charged with 114V₂ grade chlorofluorocarbon. The first shot is fired automatically, triggered by a signal from DPS-1AG flame sensors forming part of the SSP-2A fire warning system (*sistema signalizahtsü pozhahra*); the second one is activated manually.

For high-altitude operations the helicopter can be equipped with five KKO-LS oxygen equipment sets (*komplekt kislorodnovo oboroodovaniya*), each of which comprises a KP-21 breathing apparatus (*kislorodnyy pribor* – oxygen apparatus), a KP-58 breathing apparatus, a KM-16N oxygen mask (*kislorodnaya mahska*) and an R-58 connector. The flight engineer and troops transported in the cargo cabin can use portable KP-21 breathing apparatus. Three 4-litre (0.88 Imp gal) stationary oxygen bottles are fitted as standard; in CASEVAC configuration 26 additional bottles holding 7.6 litres (1.672 Imp gal) each are fitted.

*Flight and navigation equipment* includes a GMK-1A compass system, a DAK-DB-5VK celestial compass, an MRP-56P marker receiver; ARK-9 and ARK-UD automatic direction finders and an RV-3 radio altimeter. *Communications equipment* includes a two-way communications radio with an R-807 transmitter and a US-9 receiver; an R-802 command link radio; a 1-RSB-70 *Yadro-1*A (Nucleus) HF communications radio and an SPU-7U intercom; an EKSP-46 four-round signal flare launcher is provided. The *IFF system* features an SRO-2M Khrom (Chromium; *izdeliye* 023) IFF transponder. *Data recording equipment* comprises an MSRP-12 flight data recorder capturing 12 analogue parameters, including barometric altitude, indicated airspeed, roll rate, vertical and lateral G forces and throttle settings, and an MS-61 cockpit voice recorder.

An external sling device for the transportation of bulky loads can be installed in case of need. In this case a special truss carrying a swivelling lock is attached to centre fuselage mainframes 14 and 18.

Military Mi-6As feature an NUV-1M gimballed mount under the navigator's station featuring a 12.7-mm (.50 calibre) Afanas'yev A-12.7 (TKB-481) machine-gun. The normal ammunition complement is 200 rounds, the full complement is 270 rounds. The field of fire is ±30° to the sides and 55° downwards.

## ■ Mi-6A SPECIFICATIONS

| | |
|---|---|
| Length, rotors turning | 41.739 m (136 ft 11⁵⁄₃₂ in) |
| Fuselage length | 33.165 m (108 ft 9⁴⁵⁄₆₄ in) |
| Fuselage width | 3.2 m (10 ft 5⁶³⁄₆₄ in) |
| Height on ground with normal TOW, rotors stopped | 9.156 m (30 ft 0³¹⁄₆₄ in) |
| Ground angle | 2° |
| Main rotor diameter | 35.0 m (114 ft 10 in) |
| Main rotor disc area | 962 m² (10,344 sq ft) |
| Main rotor disc loading | 42.1 kg/m² (8.63 lb/sq ft) |
| Tail rotor diameter | 6.3 m (20 ft 8 in) |
| Wing span | 15.3 m (50 ft 2³⁄₄ in) |
| Wing area | 35.0 m² (376.34 sq ft) |
| Stabiliser span | 5.082 m (16 ft 8¹³⁄₆₄ in) |
| Stabiliser area | 4.87 m² (52.36 sq ft) |
| Landing gear track | 7.502 m (24 ft 7²³⁄₆₄ in) |
| Landing gear wheelbase | 9.175 m (30 ft 1⁷⁄₃₂ in) |
| Max indicated airspeed | 300 km/h (186 mph) |
| Normal take-off weight | 40,500 kg (89,285 lb) |
| Max take-off weight | 44,000 kg (97,000 lb) |
| Payload, with: | |
| 40,500-kg TOW | 5,516 kg (12,160 lb) |
| 42,500-kg (93,690-lb) TOW | 7,516 kg (16,570 lb) |
| 44,000-kg TOW | 9,016 kg (19,880 lb) |
| Max payload with a 42,500 to 44,000-kg TOW and reduced fuel | 12,000 kg (26,455 lb) |
| Max slung load | 8,000 kg (17,640 lb) |
| Service ceiling, with: | |
| normal TOW | 4,500 m (14,760 ft) |
| TOW over 40,500 kg | 3,000 m (9,840 ft) |
| Climb time with 40,500-kg TOW: | |
| to 3,000 m | 9.7 minutes |
| to 4,500 m | 20.7 minutes |
| Effective range at 1,000 m (3,280 ft) with a normal TOW | 970 km (602 miles) |
| Endurance at 1,000 m and 140-160 km/h (87-99 mph) with a normal TOW | 2.85 hours |

# The Modeller's Corner

**T**he Mi-6 is reasonably well represented on the scale model market – as of this writing, there are eight (or so) kits in three (or so) scales from no fewer than eleven (!) brands, but some of them have been out-of-stock items for ages – and some of them are definitely not worth the effort of building them.

## 1:72nd scale

In 1975 the West German manufacturer **Airmodel** released a vacuform kit of the Mi-6 (Ref. No.43, or AM-043); this was not a rebox of the East German Plastikart kit as sometimes claimed (scc below). Considering the date and the unavailability of accurate drawings or close-up photos, the accuracy of this kit left much to be desired (in particular, the windows were at the wrong locations).

A further vacuform and white metal kit of the Mi-6 (Ref. No.7219) was released in 1997 by the UK company **Sanger** (aka **Sanger-Contrail**). Its official website says this is a Welsh company based in Carmarthen, Carmarthenshire; yet the box top of the Mi-6 kit is marked 'Sanger, Bristol, UK'. The fuselage is moulded in two halves integrally with the tailboom on a huge sheet of 1.5-mm white plastic measuring about 60 x 24 cm (23⅝ in x 9²⁹⁄₆₄ in); the engine cowlings are a separate part (with inaccurate contours). Only the

doors are reproduced – there are no panel lines whatever, so the modeller has to scribe them himself. The rotor blades are hollow on the underside after separation from the sheet, so the underside has to be fabricated from plastic card. The glazing is vacuformed from clear acrylic sheet; the white metal parts comprise the landing gear (including the wheels, which are cast in halves!), the rotor hubs and control rods, the tail bumper and the engine air intakes. No decals are supplied with the kit. Well, by 1997 enough scale drawings and good photos of the helicopter were available to make a decent model possible; yet again, Sanger's Mi-6 is a rather poor resemblance.

The situation changed for the better in 2005, when the Ukrainian manufacturer **Amodel** (specialising in more or less exotic aircraft which the larger kit makers won't bother to do) took on the Mi-6. The Ukrainians were in a position to produce an accurate kit, since they knew the subject firsthand – the Ukrainian Air Force operated the Mi-6 – and accurate scale plans were available by then.

Amodel's first kit of the *Hook* (Ref. No.72119) represents the initial production Mi-6 *sans suffixe* with tapered main rotor blades and no APU; it is labelled as 'Mil Mi-6 early version'. The finished model is quite impressive, with a length of 465 mm (18¹⁹⁄₆₄ in), which is about 5 mm (0¹³⁄₆₄ in) shorter

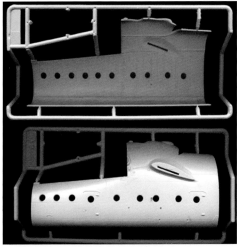

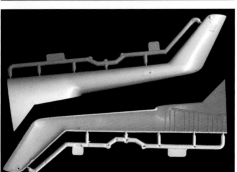

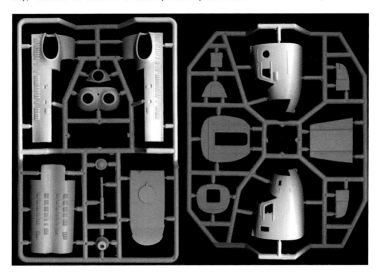

The sprues of Amodel's Mi-6 *sans suffixe* using the original tooling (with a separate flight deck section).

**Above:** The Amodel Mi-6 *sans suffixe* built by Bernhard Pethe aka 'Flugi'. The port front door was cut out and set in the open position, and replacement cabin window transparencies were manufactured; the stock handrails were replaced with copper wire and the tyres were doctored to reproduce the tread pattern. The model was painted with Xtracolor enamels.

**Opposite, top:** The sprues of Amodel's Mi-6A; note the different fuselage breakdown with an integral flight deck section.

than required, and a wing span of 215 mm (13²⁵⁄₃₂ in) – and that's not counting the rotors. Unlike some of the company's other 1:72nd scale kits of heavy aircraft (aptly dubbed 'Amonsters' because of their size and complexity), where the principal airframe components are made of glassfibre reinforced epoxy resin – commonly referred to as 'fibreglass resin' – for extra strength, here Amodel stuck to its traditional 'short run' technology. The kit consists of 175 parts; the box contains 23 sprues moulded in soft light grey polystyrene and two clear sprues. The 15-page bilingual (English/Russian) assembly instructions are quite detailed and give Humbrol enamel numbers as a painting guide. Nevertheless, this is a project for the experienced modeller, and the instruction sheet states this explicitly.

Originally the fuselage of the Amodel Mi-6 *sans suffixe* was broken down into three sections – the forward fuselage (flight

deck section), the centre fuselage (cargo cabin section) and the rear end of the cabin together with the tailboom/tail rotor pylon, each of which was split into left and right halves. A year later, when the Mi-6A kit appeared (see below), the fuselage from this kit (which has a rather different breakdown) was included into the earlier kit by way of 'reverse standardisation'; unfortunately Amodel forgot to amend the instructions accordingly, creating a puzzling discrepancy between the actual sprues and the instructions. The clamshell cargo doors (but not the entry doors) are separate parts and a reasonably well detailed cabin interior is included, giving you the option of assembling the model with the cargo doors open. The wings come in upper and lower halves.

The major airframe components have finely engraved panel lines, but some of the larger parts show a good deal of flash – a result of the 'short run' technology. Fortu-

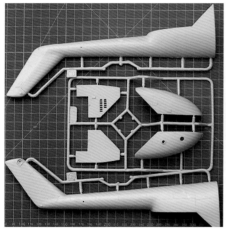
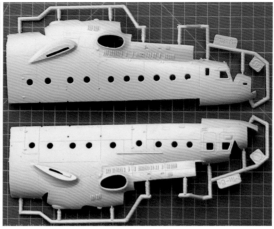

nately this problem does not affect the smaller parts, such as the detailed main rotor head, but this is inconsistent – some reviewers of the kit say the small parts are also affected. Moreover, they report that the major parts are a poor fit, with warping and sink holes here and there, and mismatching of the mould halves on the smaller parts, and a lot of putty is required; the transparencies are on the thick side – which is just as well, because they require sanding (and subsequent polishing) to achieve a proper fit.

The kit features only one decal option – a plain grey Soviet Air Force machine coded '12 Red'; the decal sheet includes instrument panels, maintenance stencils and a totally incorrect construction number which does not fit any of the four c/n systems.

**Below:** The Amodel Mi-6A built by Anatoliy Lysenko aka Rowdy to represent a Russian Air Force machine used in the First Chechen War (c/n 8683809V). The handrails and external tank attachment braces were manufactured anew from stretched sprue and the tanks were repositioned lower, the aerials from copper wire and nylon thread, the machine-gun barrel from a hypodermic needle; hydraulic and fuel lines were added, and aftermarket wheels supplied by Zebrano were used. It was painted with Gunze Sangyo acrylic paints, with pre-shading and washing, with a top coat of Micro Flat varnish.

The Amodel Mi-6A built by a modeller with the Internet alias Stanip to represent a Tyumen' CAD/Nizhnevartovsk UAD/441st Flight machine. Flight deck detail was added, the stock cargo door hinges and cowling handrails were replaced with more realistic scratchbuilt versions fashioned from plastic card and stretched sprue, and tyre tread was added. The anti-slip coating on the upper fuselage was emulated, using tissue from tea bags. The cheatline was airbrushed on and homemade decals were used; panel lines were marked with a sharp lead pencil. Note the scratchbuilt MP-85 engine heater with its fabric air hoses.

Here, again, the instruction sheet misleads the modeller by suggesting that decals are also included for a camouflaged Soviet example coded '55 Red' and a Vietnamese People's Air Force machine serialled '7809 Yellow'.

In 2006 Amodel followed up with a kit of the Mi-6A (Ref. No.72131) labelled as 'Mil Mi-6 late version'. This kit, which comprises 177 parts, incorporates the constant-chord main rotor blades, revised navigator's station glazing, revised clamshell cargo doors (with the APU air intake and jetpipe in the port one) and other subtle changes outwardly distinguishing the Mi-6A. The fuselage is split three ways – this time the flight deck and cabin sections are moulded as a single subassembly (in left and right halves), but the centre fuselage is bottomless, its underside being moulded separately. This time the parts breakdown on the instruction sheet matches the actual sprues. The decal sheet is rather more comprehensive, giving you the option of building two of the Russian Air Force Mi-6As involved in the First Chechen War – '61 Red' or '83 Red' (with correct c/ns and appropriate nose art) – or a grey-painted Aeroflot Mi-6A from the 1970s registered CCCP-21293.

## 1:100th (?) scale

The first offering to 1:100th scale on the subject – and the first kit of the Mi-6 in general – was, unsurprisingly, a Soviet kit. It was originally released in the 1960s by the Moscow-based toy factory then known as **Yoonyy tekhnik** (Young Technician) under Ref. No.MG-2262; later the factory changed its name to *Kroogozor* (Outlook) and the kit was rebranded accordingly under Ref. No.085-2262. To be precise, it was *purportedly* to 1:100th scale, though it is hard to be sure – the first Soviet plastic model kits were not consistent about scale; some sources claim the kit in question was to 1:72nd or even 1:120th scale. The crude cardboard box featured a fairly accurate drawing of the Mi-6P 'helibus', albeit with spats on all three landing gear units which the real Mi-6P did not have; the model itself, however, represented

the Mi-6A with circular windows. Inside were 32 parts injection-moulded in plastic of assorted colours (plus a two-piece display stand) and a decal sheet with nothing but a fictitious registration and the Soviet flag. The fuselage, which was moulded in two halves integrally with the tailboom and tail rotor pylon, had raised panel lines and the aircraft type was marked on the nose (!). The moulds were made of substandard metal and had to be repaired every now and then; as a result, the castings had quite a bit of flash. While the overall proportions were more or less correct, the contours were not; moreover, the kit did not include any transparencies, the windows being emulated by raised lines (in the crew section) or recesses (in the cabin) which had to be coloured in after assembly. In other words, this was more of a toy than a proper

model kit; the verdict issued at one of the Russian scale modelling websites was: 'Retro? This ain't retro, this is for the sandbox!' According to some sources, the kit was later reboxed under the **Diwi** brand (Ref. No.218).

In 1965, when a cutaway model of the Mi-6P (then still at the project stage) was displayed at an aviation event at Moscow-Vnukovo airport, it attracted the attention of East German specialists. A plastic kit manufacturer, then known as **KVZ (VEB Kunststoff-Verarbeitung Zschopau** – 'Zschopau Plastic Processing Co. – People's Enterprise') was operating since 1958 in the town of Zschopau, in what was then the Karl-Marx-Stadt District of southern East Germany (this became part of the federal state of Saxony after German reunification). Someone decided that KVZ should produce a kit of the Mi-6, and the moulds were ready in a few months – before the real Mi-6P had even flown. Thus, *running ahead of the steam engine* (to use a Russian colloquial expression), the Germans ended up with *a model of a model*. Haste makes waste: first released in 1967, the KVZ Mi-6 kit (Ref. No.5014) was a total disaster. Oh, to be sure, the surface finish and the packaging were way better than the Kroogozor kit, but the model itself was wildly inaccurate (like most other products from this particular manufacturer). The proportions and outlines were completely wrong, there were 15 cabin windows on each side and only one door instead of 12 windows per side and three doors, there were no external fuel tanks and so on (never mind the suggested colour scheme and the registration CCCP-37140, which in fact belonged to an Antonov An-2 utility biplane!). To this day, modellers disagree even on the scale of the East German kit; the manufacturer billed it as 1:100th scale, but many suggest it is more like 1:87th (a popular model railway scale) or 1:75th scale. There have even been claims that the model itself is to 1:87th scale while the main rotor is to 1:100th scale!

The box featured colourful artwork and contained three sprues cast in gloss white plastic, one sprue cast in gloss black plastic, one clear sprue, a very basic decal sheet, a small glass jar of liquid cement and a small glass jar of silver paint. The fuselage halves had engraved panel lines. All in all, there were 90 parts (including a few spare cabin window transparencies) plus a two-piece display stand. The plastic was very hard and brittle, requiring care when separating the parts from the sprues. The assembly instructions were in German, Russian, Czech and Polish, plus an occasional English-language leaflet added.

Over the years the Mi-6 kit was released under a variety of brands. First, the company changed its name to **MPKAB (VEB Modell- und Plastspielwaren-Kombinat Annaberg-Buchholz** – 'Annaberg-Buchholz Model & Plastic Toy Factory'), being officially based in the town of Annaberg-Buchholz in the same district in 1969-73; from 1973 to

The Yoonyy Tekhnik 1:100th scale Mi-6 built out of the box by Yuriy Zaslavskiy (who lists it as 1:72nd scale). The model was painted with a mixture of aluminium powder and nitrocellulose varnish; the decals were sourced from the spares box as the stock ones were unusable.

The original box art of the Mi-6 kit issued by KVZ; and the same kit reissued under the VEB Plasticart brand, the box art shows an Mi-6 over the oil rigs of the Neftyanyye Kamni ('Oil Stones') oilfield in the Caspian Sea near Baku.

1989 the company did business as **VEB Plasticart Zschopau**, and it is under the Plasticart Modelle brand that the Mi-6 kit is best known (as Ref. No.15080). In an effort to earn hard currency, in the 1980s the Plasticart Mi-6 kit was reboxed for the western market under two brands – **Nu-Bee** (labelled as 'Civil Helicopter Mi-6') and **Playfix Kits** (Ref. No.670, labelled as 'Giant Soviet Helicopter', as simple as that); these were distributed via a UK importer. After German reunification Plasticart was privatised and rebranded **adp Master-Modell**, carrying on with the same range of models until it finally

**Above:** The latest incarnation of the KVZ/Plasticart kit released by reifra Kunststofftechnik.

**Right:** The sprues of the Plasticart Mi-6. Note the way too many windows and the absolutely incorrect contours.

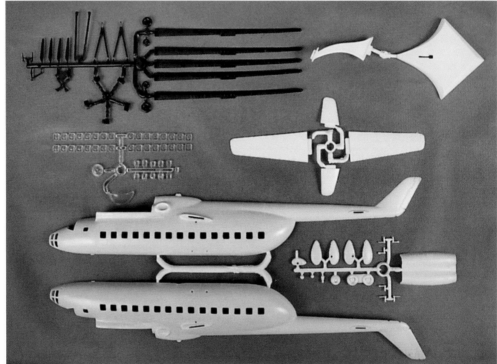

**Below and opposite page, top:** The Plasticart Mi-6 built out of the box by Yuriy Lazarev from Karaganda, Kazakhstan.

went bankrupt (the Mi-6 kit was Ref. No.1003). Yet the models refused to die – the moulds were acquired by the Polish company **Wojar** (pronounced '*voyar*') based in Oleśnica, which produced the Mi-6 kit for a while (Ref. No.99031). Most recently, in 2012, the ex-Plasticart kits were reissued by the German company **reifra Kunststofftechnik** (likewise based in Annaberg-Buchholz); the Mi-6 kit (Ref. No.S13007011)

differs from the original version only in the box art and the use of a less glossy plastic for the white sprues – even the decals and the instructions are the same. 'A rose by any other name...' Well, the same is true for *not a rose*. The moulds have been refurbished, however, and one of the sprues (with the wings and stabilisers), which used to be cruciform, now looks suspiciously like a swastika...

## 1:144th scale

At this end of the range we again have quite a selection. First, the British manufacturer **Air Craft Models**, which went out of business in 1997, released a vacuform/white metal kit of the Mi-6 (Ref. No.421). Next, in 2010 the company **LEM Models** (makes you wonder if LEM stands for 'limited edition models') issued a kit of the Mi-6A cast in polyester resin. The kit consists of 45 parts and the airframe breakdown is almost like that of the real thing (forward fuselage, centre fuselage, engine cowlings/air intakes, tailboom/tail rotor pylon, wings and stabilisers). The fuselage sections are hollow cast, the flight deck glazing is partly vacuformed and the landing gear struts are cast in white metal, albeit with a good deal of flash; wire inserts are included for attaching the main rotor blades to the rotor head. Decals are provided for Soviet/Russian Air Force and Ukrainian Army Aviation examples. Judging by the fact that the kit comes complete with a copy of the scale plans from the Mi-6 monographic feature in the Ukrainian magazine *Aviatsiya i Vremya* (Aviation & Time) No.1-1999, these were the ones used for making the master model, which means the kit is accurate enough. On the other hand, resin kits are not for the beginner; also, the kit is now rare.

Thirdly, in 2013 the Russian 'short run' kit manufacturer **Eastern Express/Vos-**

**tochnyy Ekspress** let loose with three kits of the subject. The Mi-6 *sans suffixe* (Ref. No.14506) – labelled as 'Heavy Multi-Purpose Helicopter Mi-6 early version' – features decals for building Soviet Air Force machines coded '02 Blue' or '19 Red' (with incorrect c/ns, unfortunately). The Mi-6A (labelled as 'Heavy Multi-Purpose Helicopter Mi-6 late version') is available in two versions with different decals by the Russian manufacturer Begemot Decals. One (Ref. No.14507) lets you build any of two Soviet Air Force machines ('01 Red' and '84 Red',

The box top of the Eastern Express Mi-6 *sans suffixe*.

The box tops of the Eastern Express Mi-6A in both military and civil guise.

The sprues of the Eastern Express Mi-6A. Note the absence of the cabin windows, which need to be drilled out – unless you choose to simulate them, using the decals.

the latter is a SAR helicopter), two Russian Air Force machines used in the First Chechen War (the aforementioned '61 Red' and '83 Red') and a Russian Navy machine coded '12 Yellow'. The other (Ref. No.14508) gives a choice of three Aeroflot machines – CCCP-21868 in Air Force-style overall grey, CCCP-06174 in a smart blue/white 1970s demonstrator scheme and RA-21030 in 1973-standard orange/blue livery for Polar regions.

The kits basically match the scale plans in the abovementioned issue of *Aviatsiya i Vremya*, albeit the tail rotor blades are a bit on the short side. The kit comprises 111

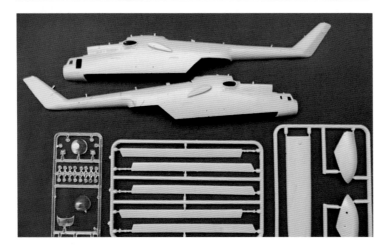

parts on four sprues moulded in light grey plastic and one clear sprue; the latter includes alternative navigator's station glazing parts for the two versions. Eastern express is noted for inconsistency in manufacturing standards, and, judging by the negative feedback from modellers, the Mi-6 kits are not among their best-quality products.

The fuselage breakdown is similar to Amodel's Mi-6A kit (except that there is no transverse break, the tailboom being moulded integrally) – that is, the centre fuselage underside is moulded separately because the panel lines there are different on the Mi-6 *sans suffixe* and the Mi-6A. Again, the clamshell cargo doors (and the flight deck escape hatch to port, because it differs on the two versions, but not the entry doors) are separate parts but there is no hint of a cabin interior, which will have to be scratchbuilt if you wish to leave the doors open. Moreover, the cabin windows are not even apertures – they are merely marked on the fuselage halves, and the instructions suggest drilling them out with a 2.7-mm drill if you want to use the cabin window transparencies! As an alternative, all windows are provided as dark shapes on the decal sheet.

## 1:300th scale

This one deserves mention only as a curio, since it is not a proper model kit. The now-defunct British company **Skytrex Models**, which catered for railway modellers and wargamers, released a 1:300th scale (also described as 6-mm scale) white metal kit of the Mi-6 (Ref. No.SMA 900) consisting of five parts – fuselage, tailboom, wings and the main gear units stuck together on a common axle. However, the metal miniature turned out to be really worthless – it was just a lump of metal that did not capture the appearance of the Mi-6 at all (one reviewer described it as 'I am sorry to say but you really want to stay away from that particular model').

## AFTERMARKET ITEMS

Those who are not content with building the Mi-6 'out of the box' and wish to add something extra will be in for a disappointment – there are very few accessories for the *Hook*. The Czech company **Extra Tech** released a set of photo-etched (PE) exterior and interior parts (Ref. No.EX 14410) for the 1:72nd scale Amodel kits; the Belorussian company **Zebrano** has a set of weighted resin wheels with the correct tread pattern for same (Ref. No.ZA72201), while the Russian company **Equipage** offers a set of resin/rubber wheels for the 1:144th scale kits. And that's about it, so if you want more, it will mostly be a DIY job!

# Mi-26:
# Next-generation 'Big Lifter'

**B**y the early 1970s the complexity and scope of the tasks to be tackled by the Soviet Union's helicopter fleet had grown considerably, and the Mi-6 proved incapable of meeting them to the full. An increasing need arose for transporting bulky cargoes weighing up to 20 tons (44,000 lb), such as new weaponry types for mechanised infantry divisions, over distances of up to 800 km (500 miles); importantly, the localities of eventual operations could be as high as 1,500 m (4,900 ft) above sea level. Therefore, headed by Chief Designer Marat N. Tishchenko since 1970, the Mil' Moscow Helicopter Plant named after Mikhail L. Mil' (MVZ – *Moskovskiy vertolyotnyy zavod*, as OKB-329 was named after its founder's death) embarked on the design of new-generation heavy-lift helicopters. At the same time the V-12 programme was wound up due to the cancellation of the ballistic missile system which the V-12 was meant to transport.

Chief Designer G. P. Smirnov and his deputy Aleksey G. Samoosenko exercised voverall control of the new programme, while O. P. Bakhov was the project chief. At first the designers tried to make maximum use of production components from the Mi-6 and a number of technical features evolved earlier. Several layouts were considered, including a side-by-side twin rotor layout and a tandem twin-rotor layout; the latter appeared to offer some advantages, such as the reduction of the rotor diameter, allowing the rotors and gearboxes to be made smaller and lighter. However, studies revealed that in the long run a tandem-rotor helicopter would be a considerably heavier and more complex machine; also, the intention to use components from earlier helicopters and resort to previously tried design methods would hardly lead to success. Hence, after joint research with the Central Aero-and Hydrodynamics Institute named after Nikolay Ye. Zhukovskiy (TsAGI – *Tsentrahl'nyy aero- i ghidrodinamicheskiy institoot*) and the Central Aero Engine Institute (TsIAM – *Tsentrahl'nyy institoot aviatsionnovo motorostroyeniya*), the designers chose to stick with the single-rotor layout. The new-generation heavy-lift helicopter was allocated the designation **Mi-26** and the product code *izdeliye* 90. The PD project was approved by the Scientific & Technical Council of the Ministry of Aircraft Industry in December 1971.

In accordance with the MoD's operational requirements the helicopter was to transport cargoes weighing up to 20 tons (44,000 lb) over a distance of 400 km (250 miles), while having a hovering ceiling in excess of 1,500 m (4,900 ft). A powerplant with a total output of no less than 20,000 shp was needed to attain these performance figures. The designers opted for two 11,400-eshp D-136 turboshafts then under development at the 'Progress' Zaporozhye Engine Design Bureau (ZMKB *'Progress' – Zaporozhskoye motorno-konstrooktorskoye byuro*, formerly OKB-478) headed by Vladimir A. Lotarev. The D-136 was based on the core of the D-36 turbofan and featured a modular design incorporating devices for early detection of failures; Chief Designer Fyodor M. Muravchenko led the design effort. The powerplant was to feature an integral system automatically maintaining the required main rotor RPM and harmonising the power of the two engines. In the event of a single-engine failure the good engine would automatically go to contingency rating, enabling the helicopter to continue climbing and to hover in ground effect – providing the all-up weight did not exceed 40 tons (88,200 lb).

A ground test rig at the Mil' OKB's flight test facility in Panki with the Mi-26 static test article

CCCP-06141, the first prototype Mi-26, seen during trials with a non-standard air data boom. Note the strakes on the clamshell cargo doors – a feature unique to this machine.

The VR-26 main gearbox (*vertolyotnyy redooktor* – helicopter gearbox) was developed in-house; previously the main gearboxes of Mil' helicopters had been developed by the engine makers. The designers relinquished the planetary layout in favour of a radically new three-cascade layout. This, coupled with other new features, allowed the VR-26 to transmit to the main rotor twice the power and 50% greater torque compared to the Mi-6's R-7 at the cost of an insignificant weight penalty.

The Mil' OKB paid much attention to selecting the optimum parameters of the rotor system. Following joint research work with TsAGI, they developed highly efficient main rotor blades of metal and glassfibre construction. The eight-blade rotor had a diameter of 28 m (91 ft 10½ in) and was 40% lighter than the Mi-6's five-blade rotor. For the first time the rotor head was made of titanium alloy which ensured great fatigue strength and a 15% weight reduction as compared to the Mi-6's steel rotor head.

The first prototype runs up the engines. Note the open APU air intake louvers.

Equally innovative was the design of the five-blade tail rotor having all-glassfibre blades; it developed twice the thrust and had a 1.4 m (4 ft 7⅛ in) greater diameter while retaining the same weight as the Mi-6's tail rotor.

When projecting the Mi-26, the designers used the operational experience gained with its predecessor to the full. For example, the engine air intakes were provided with vortex-type dust/debris filters separating 65-70% of the dust, reducing wear and tear on the engines in dusty localities virtually without detriment to power output. To facilitate maintenance, not only did the engine cowling panels double as work platforms but a crawlway to the tail rotor was provided inside the tailboom and the tail rotor pylon. Furthermore, to facilitate loading and unloading the Mi-26 featured two electric winches and an overhead gantry crane with a lifting capacity of up to 5 tons (11,025 lb). The rear loading hatch was closed by clamshell doors and a hydraulically actuated cargo ramp; the latter could be fixed in a horizontal position, allowing the helicopter to carry items of outsize length, or in a position allowing straight-in loading from a truck bed. The main undercarriage units made it possible to change the ground clearance of the parked helicopter and align the load with the cargo ramp. The external suspension system enabled the helicopter to carry slung loads weighing up to 20 tons (44,100 lb).

The Mi-26's cabin could accommodate 70 paratroopers or 85 soldiers with full kit. The helicopter could be outfitted for CASEVAC duties within a few hours to accommodate 60 stretcher patients and three medical attendants.

The avionics suite included a weather radar allowing the Mi-26 to operate around the clock in visual and instrument weather conditions. The flight control system incorporated a three-channel autopilot, systems for trajectory and flight director control; there was also a voice warning system informing the crew of emergency situations in flight.

Construction of the full-size mock-up of the Mi-26 started in 1972; by the time it was approved by the mock-up review commission in 1975 the design work was largely completed. Registered CCCP-06141, the first prototype (c/n 00-01) was rolled out at the Mil' OKB's experimental production facility in Panki in October 1977. On 14th December, after six weeks of ground tests, the Mi-26 performed its first hover, captained by project test pilot Gurghen R. Karapetyan. In February 1978 the helicopter was ferried to the OKB's flight test facility in Lyubertsy just south-east of Moscow where the main part of the manufacturer's tests was conducted.

CCCP-06141 lifts off at the Mil' OKB's flight test facility in Panki in December 1977.

A fine study of CCCP-06141 in later guise with a non-standard red radome.

One of the Mi-26 prototypes and its crew at a mountain airfield during tests.

**Right:** The first prototype seen in the 1990s as RA-06141 in service with the OKB's own 'airline' Mi-Avia. The strakes are gone; note the addition of external reinforcement ribs on the rear fuselage and the tailboom.

**Below:** The changing of the guard: seen here with a Mi-6 at Kubinka in 1991, the Mi-26 illustrates the generation change in Soviet heavy helicopter design.

**Opposite page:** Still new and shiny, Mi-26 '09 Yellow' illustrates the type's standard camouflage in Soviet/CIS military service. Interestingly, most of the military Mi-26s have yellow codes.

The Mi-26 passed joint state acceptance trials at GNIKI VVS between May 1979 and August 1980. In the course of the trials CCCP-06141 and the second prototype (CCCP-06140, c/n 00-02), which was also built at Panki, performed a total of 150 flights, logging 104 flight hours between them; no problems worthy of note were encountered. As a result, the Mi-26 was recommended for production and for Soviet Army service. CCCP-06141 eventually gained Soviet Air Force camouflage and star insignia, becoming '01 Yellow'. CCCP-06140 had an unhappy fate, crashing near Choporovo village (Yaroslavl' Region) on 13th December 1989 when the control system failed; the crew of five captained by test pilot Anatoliy P. Razbegayev were killed.

Plant No.168, aka Rostov Helicopter Production Enterprise (RVPP – *Rostovskoye vertolyotostroitel'noye proizvodstvennoye predpriyatiye*), began tooling up for Mi-26 production in 1976, when the trials were still

in progress. Officially the helicopter entered production on 4th October 1977.

Concurrently the *Motorostroitel'* (= Engine Manufacturer) Production Association in Zaporozhye, the Ukraine (formerly plant No.478; now called Motor-Sich Joint-Stock Co.) launched production of the D-136 turboshaft. The engine proved to be very successful; in addition to a very high power rating, it featured a low SFC of only 9.206 kg/ehp (20.29 lb/ehp). Coupled with the helicopter's excellent aerodynamics, this made it possible to obtain an unprecedentedly low fuel burn per tonne of payload.

On 4th October 1980 the first production Mi-26 (c/n 34001212001; fuselage number 0101 – that is, Batch 01, 01st aircraft in the batch) was rolled out at Rostov-on-Don/Krestovka – the factory airfield of plant No. 168. The first hover took place at noon on 25th October, after lengthy ground checks; it was followed by a circuit flight on 26th October. In both cases the helicopter was flown by

an MVZ Mil' test crew captained by Gurghen R. Karapetyan. Further tests of the first production Mi-26 were conducted jointly by crews from the Rostov plant and the Air Force. (Note: Production Mi-26s normally have 11-digit construction numbers. The first eight digits are invariably 34001212, 340 being a code for the Rostov factory; the last three are individual and allocated in large sequential blocks – although there are gaps in the sequence to confuse would-be spies. Additionally, 17 export examples, including those diverted to the Russian market due to arms embargoes, have six-digit export c/ns; the first three digits are a customer code, followed by a 2 and the sequence number of the export airframe.)

The testing of production machines did not always run smoothly. For example, Mi-26 c/n 34001212013 (f/n 0303) operated by the Flight Research Institute named after Mikhail M. Gromov (LII – **Lyot**no-is**sle**-**dovatel'skiy institoot**) crashed at an industrial airfield known by the callsign Kazbek on 8th July 1987. A landing approach with an excessively nose-high attitude ended in a tailstrike, whereupon the tailboom broke off, the helicopter rolled over on its starboard side and was destroyed by the ensuing fire. On another occasion a test flight with the objective of developing the rolling landing technique on a fully fuelled helicopter with one engine inoperative ended in a crash in almost identical circumstances. Luckily the crew survived in both cases. After this, recommendations were evolved for improving the landing gear shock absorbers and reinforcing the tailboom.

Production Mi-26s were intended primarily for equipping the helicopter regiments of the Air Force; deliveries to Aeroflot ranked second in importance. The military version differed from the civil configuration in being equipped with chaff/flare dispensers in prominent fairings on the fuselage sides and mounts for hand-held weapons at the cargo cabin windows. Soviet Air Force Mi-26s were delivered in a two-tone green camouflage scheme.

Full-scale deliveries of the Mi-26 had not yet started when the helicopter established a series of world records. For example, on 4th February 1982 a Mi-26 captained by test pilot Gherman V. Alfyorov lifted a payload of 25 tons (55,125 lb) to an altitude of 4,060 m (13,320 ft) and climbed to 2,000 m (6,560 ft) at an all-up weight of 56,768.8 kg (125,151.6 lb). That same year a Mi-26 crew captained by woman pilot Inna A. Kopets set nine world records for women. When the machine was already in widespread service, a GNIKI VVS crew headed by Anatoliy P. Razbegayev beat a world speed record that had been set by the Mi-8 back in 1967; on 7th August 1988 they averaged 279 km/h (173 mph) over a 2,000-km (1,242-mile) closed-circuit route.

A notable contribution to the Mi-26's development was made by LII test pilots. For example, in 1986 the institute evolved a technique of transporting an outsize slung cargo weighing 37 tons (81,570 lb) by two helicopters. During one of the flights a faulty external sling on the helicopter captained by Arkadiy P. Makarov broke away. This was fraught with the danger of a crash for the second helicopter captained by Anatoliy D. Grishchenko; tragedy was averted thanks to the instant reaction of co-pilot Vladimir P. Somov who jettisoned the cargo. That marked the end of the unique experimental job. Much later, by 1998, LII had completed a comprehensive flight test programme to assess the Mi-26's structural loads within the permitted speed envelope, determine the longitudinal stability and control characteristics and study the machine's behaviour during autorotation landings. This research was intended to enhance the helicopter's operational capabilities.

The Mi-26 was shown to the general public for the first time in June 1981 at the 34th Paris Air Show where it became the star of the show. It was allocated the NATO reporting name *Halo*.

On 12th January 1985 a civil version of the helicopter designated **Mi-26T** (**trahn-sportnyy** – transport, used attributively) was put into production. The commercial version differed from the basic military Mi-26 *sans suffixe* primarily in the navigation avionics; it lacked the lateral chaff/flare dispensers and the mounts for assault rifles. The complement of equipment designed to enhance the machine's capabilities for operating with slung loads was considerably increased. For example, an azimuth orientation system ensured the optimum position of the slung load in cruise flight and its orientation in the hover; a system for damping oscillations through the autopilot counteracted the possible swinging of the load. An electronic weight measurement system determined the weight of the load in the hover with an error margin of 1%; the machine featured DG-65 or VTDG-20 electrically operated locks making it possible to disengage the load without assistance from ground personnel. An external suspension system fitted with a spreader bar allowed the Mi-26T to carry standard sea/land containers without assistance from cargo handling personnel. A device called versatile stabilising platform (USP – *ooniver**sahl**'naya stabili**zee**ruyushchaya plat**for**ma*) made it possible to increase the flight speed with bulky elongated items (such as a prefabricated cabin, a container, a pipe) on a sling to 200 km/h (124 mph) and reduces the fuel consumption by up to 50%. In addition, the range of cargo handling devices utilised by the Mi-26 was supplemented by an automatic grip for handling large-diameter oil and gas pipes and a grip for heli-logging operations in mountainous areas. Mi-26T production for Aeroflot began with CCCP-06001 (c/n 34001212084, f/n 0801) which was released by the factory on 26th December 1985.

The next stage in the helicopter's improvement was to incorporate measures enhancing operational reliability and surviv-

CCCP-06008, one of the first examples of the Mi-26T civil version.

ability. For instance, the aluminium push-pull rods in the flight control system were replaced by steel rods to reduce the risk of their melting in the event of an in-flight fire, with an ensuing loss of control. In this guise the machine was certified by the Air Register of the CIS Interstate Aviation Committee in accordance with the Russian NLGV-2 airworthiness regulations for helicopters (*Normy lyotnoy godnosti vertolyotov*), which are harmonised with the American FAR-29 regulations. On 27th September 1995 the new baseline version received the designation **Mi-26TS** (*sertifitseerovannyy* – certified); in advertising materials for the export market, however, the helicopter is referred to as the **Mi-26TC**. The prototype of this version was probably RA-29112, a Mi-26T owned by the Rostov plant (c/n 34001212407, export c/n 226210, f/n 1807).

Tests were conducted of the **Mi-26A** equipped with a new flight and navigation avionics suite. The machine remained a prototype.

In the early 2000s MVZ and Rostvertol considered equipping the Mi-26 with state-of-the-art avionics, which would allow the flight crew to be reduced to two pilots, automating away the navigator and the flight engineer; a third crew member would still be carried during operations with slung loads. Designated **Mi-26T2**, the helicopter was to have an NPK-90-2 advanced flight/navigation suite including an electronic flight instrumentation system ('glass cockpit') with five multi-function displays and an electro-optical surveillance system in a gyrostabilised undernose turret; the avionics would include a moving-map display (MMD), a modern weather radar, a system for precision flight control in the hover, night-vision goggles and so on. Furthermore, introduction of a health and usage monitoring system (HUMS) would cut maintenance man-hours

Mi-26T RA-06041 being used for a humanitarian mission in MEDEVAC configuration with red cross/red crescent markings.

Mi-26TS RA-06295 in the striking red/white livery of the Moscow City Fire Department.

A mock-up version of the Mi-26T2's flight deck featuring an electronic flight instrumentation system.

The still-unmarked Mi-26T2 prototype test flying from Rostov-on-Don/Krestovka in the spring of 2012.

the form of a working flight deck mock-up; the same mock-up was later demonstrated at the MAKS-2003 airshow (19th-24th August 2003). According to the estimates of western experts, *'the upgraded Mi-26T2 could fetch between $15 million and $18 million on the world market, whereas the standard Mi-26 costs from $11 million to $13 million'*.

The Mi-26T2 prototype was converted by Rostvertol from an early-production Russian Air Force machine coded '56 Yellow' (c/n 34001212096, f/n 0901). Painted light grey overall with Mil' and Rostvertol logos, the then-uncoded helicopter was rolled out in late December 2010, making its first flight on 22nd February 2011; it was subsequently coded '901 Black'. The actual Mi-26T2 had no EO turret; instead, a powerful searchlight was fitted under the nose. In August the upgraded helicopter made its public debut at the MAKS-2011 airshow. Rostvertol General Director Boris Slyusar' stated in February 2012 that the Mi-26T2 would enter production in 2012 to become the new baseline version; however, these plans turned out to be overly optimistic, and production entry is now planned for 2015.

Speaking of production, so far the production run of the Mi-26 is 314 (including the Moscow-built prototypes and static test airframe), and counting. A large proportion of this number was delivered to military customers at home and abroad. Production peaked in 1990 when 38 Mi-26s were built; on the other hand, there were years when not a single Mi-26 was produced.

by some 20%. These measures appeared certain to make the Mi-26 more attractive for potential customers.

The Mi-26T2 upgrade was unveiled at the Farnborough International 2002 airshow in

Now coded '901 Black', the Mi-26T2 prototype makes a demonstration flight at the MAKS-2013 airshow in Zhukovskiy.

The flight deck of the Mi-26T2 as actually built, showing the six multi-function displays.

# Special Versions and Unbuilt Projects

The Mi-26 turned out to be an extremely versatile helicopter, and several lines along which more or less specialised versions were developed can be singled out. The first of these, quite naturally, was the enhancement of the helicopter's potential for performing as a 'flying crane'. The Rostvertol Joint-Stock Co. (as the plant was renamed in 1992) developed a version designated **Mi-26TM** (*modifit-seerovannyy* – modified) and fitted with an additional cockpit for the pilot/operator offering a good downward view to allow accurate positioning of the cargo during construction work. Two alternative configurations of the Mi-26TM were offered; in the first one a glazed ventral 'bathtub' with a set of controls mechanically linked to the standard control runs was installed between centre fuselage frames 3-5, the pilot facing aft. The company-owned Mi-26TM prototype with the ventral cockpit, RA-06089 (c/n 34001212499, f/n 2508) made its first flight on 13th November 1992; on 30th August/5th September 1993 this machine was displayed at the MAKS-93 airshow in Zhukovskiy.

The second version had a sloping structure with a forward-facing rear cockpit fitted in place of the standard cargo ramp (the clamshell doors were retained). The additional cockpit featured fly-by-wire controls and was provided with jettisonable side blisters allowing rapid escape in an emergency; it was publicly unveiled in mock-up form at the MosAeroShow '92 – Russia's first international airshow held at Zhukovskiy on 11th-16th August 1992. The prototype of the version with the rear cockpit (-06088) flew on 15th October 1993. Apparently no more Mi-26s were thus modified.

In Moscow the initiative of the Rostov factory was frowned upon – obviously because the head office had a competing project of its own in the making. In 1997 MVZ Mil' offered its own 'flying crane' modification designated **Mi-26PK** (*podvesnaya kabina* – suspended cockpit). Quite simply, a glazed external cubicle with an aft-facing seat was installed in place of the port forward entry door; it was fitted with a set of controls mechanically linked to the existing ones. The Mi-26PK prototype was converted from the abovementioned Mi-26TM RA-06089, appearing in the static park of the MAKS-97 airshow. Apart from the addition of the port side cockpit, the machine had a device looking like a cathode-ray tube (CRT) display in a boxy housing installed on the port side of the nose immediately ahead of the captain's windscreen. Four years later a Russian Air Force Mi-26 coded '80 Yellow' (c/n 34001212081, f/n 0708) was in the static park at the MAKS-2001 airshow, featuring an identical external cockpit but lacking the device on the nose seen earlier on RA-06089; it sported the logo of the Vzlyot (Take-off) specialised air services enterprise which operated the helicopter. A similar external control cubicle found use on Mi-26T RA-06146 operated by Aerinn Heli Harvest; this time it was scabbed on to the starboard side of the flight deck and had a more rounded shape.

For several years MVZ worked on a project for a radical redesign of the *Halo* – the **Mi-26K** (*krahn* – crane) with a crew of six. It bore a striking likeness to the Sikorsky S-64 Skycrane (CH-54), the existing crew section being mated with a new slender fuselage and tall kinked main gear units closely resembling those of the Skycrane. The machine was to

Mi-26 -06088 (the CCCP prefix has been painted out) equipped with an aft control station supplanting the cargo doors/ramp as the Mi-26TM flying crane.

have a maximum take-of weight of 54 tons (119,000 lb), a maximum payload of 25 tons (55,125 lb), a cruising speed of 200 km/h (124 mph) with a slung load, a range of 520 km (323 miles) with a 17-ton (37,500-lb) payload and a hovering ceiling of 1,800 m (5,900 ft). There were plans for putting the Mi-26K into production in 1996, yet not even a prototype was been built because the Russian economy was then in the throes of a crisis.

The second line of development was fire-fighting. On 16th August 1994 the **Mi-26TP** prototype (the P stood for *pozharnyy* – fire-fighting) made its first flight in Rostov. It was intended for fighting fires in all types of local-ities, including industrial sites, and deliver-ing fire-fighting teams with their various special equipment. The helicopter's mission equipment comprised an operator's work-station, four water tanks with a total capac-ity of 15 m³ (529.7 cu ft), two reservoirs for fire retardant or foaming agent with a total capacity of 0.9 m³ (31.78 cu ft), a system for pressurising these tanks to a level of 1.4 kg/cm² (20 psi), a system for dosing the chemical agents fed to the water tanks and a manifold for discharging the liquid through the standard external sling hatch. The water tanks could be emptied in 35-45 seconds and refilled on the ground in just two minutes. The helicopter also featured a thermal imaging device, a satellite naviga-tion system, means of individual protection for the crew and radios for communication with the fire-fighting teams on the ground. Rostvertol engineers claimed that any Mi-26 could be outfitted as a Mi-26TP water-bomber in just one hour.

A different fire-fighting version tested by Rostvertol involved equipping the Mi-26 **with two externally slung EP-8000 tanks** carried on a 60-m (197-ft) suspension sys-tem. This version did not seem to hold much promise because a mobile refilling station was required for filling the tanks with water. A much more attractive option was to fit the Mi-26 **with so-called Twin Bambi Bucket flexible tanks** holding a total of 15 tons (33,000 lb) of water. With them, the helicop-ter could deliver 19,600 litres (4,312 Imp gal) of water to the fire in one pass. Electric remote controls allowed the tanks to be dis-charged in a 'salvo' or consecutively. Tests involving a Mi-26TS belonging to Krasnodar-based NII PANKh (*Naoochno-issle-dovatel'skiy institoot primeneniya aviahtsii v narodnom khozyaistve* – Research Insti-tute for the Use of Aviation in the National Economy) and equipped with Twin Bambi Buckets were conducted near *stanitsa* (Cossack village) Lazarevskaya, Krasnodar Territory, in 1997. The helicopter was stable with this load at speeds up to 227 km/h (141 mph). The system found use on a Mi-26T delivered to South Korea in 1997.

On 17th September 1997 yet another fire-fighting version of the Mi-26 performed its first flight from Rostov. It was equipped **with the indigenous VSU-15 'Bambi**

Close-up of the Mi-26TM's aft control station in a slightly different version (note that the clamshell doors have been retained in this case).

Another configuration of the Mi-26TM with an aft-looking 'bathtub' additional control station.

The external control cubicle of Mi-26PK '80 Yellow' displayed at the MAKS-2001 airshow.

Mi-26T RA-06146 operated by Aerinn Heli Harvest (and named 'Vova') with an external control cubicle on the starboard side of the flight deck.

Bucket' (**vod**oslivn**oye** oostroystvo – water discharge device) with a capacity of 15 m³ (529.7 cu ft). This device was designed, manufactured and tested by the St. Petersburg-based Technoex company jointly with NPK PANKh (ex-NII PANKh; NPK = *Na**ooch**no-proiz**vod**stvennyy **kom**pleks* – Science & Production Complex). It can be replenished from any open body of water in the hover in about 10 seconds; the discharge of the water takes 15 seconds. In 1998 the VSU-15 was put into production, becoming standard equipment for Mi-26Ts operated by the Russian Ministry for Civil Aid and Protection (EMERCOM of Russia). One Mi-26TS thus equipped, RA-06285 (c/n 34001212511, f/n 2610) was delivered to the Moscow City Fire Department in 1999 (the fire departments have since come under EMERCOM control).

As early as 1988 MVZ Mil' developed a refuelling tanker version of the Mi-26 designated **Mi-26TZ** (**top**livoza**prav**shchik) as a successor to the Mi-6TZ. However, it was not until 1st February 1996 that the production version incorporating some changes introduced by Rostvertol took to the air at Rostov-on-Don/Krestovka. Its mission is urgent delivery of fuel and refuelling of various military vehicles, including aircraft. The cargo cabin houses modular refuelling equipment which comprises two trolleys with fuel tanks, pump units and control panels, trolleys with four distribution hoses for aviation fuel, ten hoses for diesel fuel and fuel transfer meters. The volume of the fuel carried is 14,000 litres (3,080 Imp gal), the volume of lubricants is 1,040 litres (228.8 Imp gal) – that is, fifty-two 20-litre (4.4 Imp gal) jerrycans. Conversion time from a regular Mi-26 is 1 hour 25 minutes; the time required for deployment of the equipment and the reverse procedure is 10 to 25 minutes. The tanks intended for the refuelling mission can also be used as ferry tanks for extending the helicopter's range. A small number of such machines was built at Rostvertol; six have been identified to date.

Among the one-off versions was the **Mi-26P** (the first thus designated), the P suffix denoting *pogra**nich**nyy* – Border Guard

version. It was intended for use by the KGB's Border Guard troops in the High North and was fitted with a special communications equipment suite.

In 1990 a single production Mi-26 (CCCP-06146, c/n 34001212317, f/n 1610) was converted into the **Mi-26NEF-M** ASW helicopter prototype equipped with a dunking sonar; *nef* – Russian for 'nave' – was probably the codename of the mission equipment suite. The machine's main external distinguishing feature was the curiously drooping 'tapir snout' housing a 360° search radar instead of the usual weather radar. A towed magnetic anomaly detector (MAD) 'bird' was located under the non-functional rear clamshell doors; two bulges over as-yet unidentified equipment were positioned on the fuselage sides above the chaff/flare dispensers. Apparently the mission equipment was developed by the Leningrad-based LNPO Leninets (*Leningrahdskoye naoochno-proizvodstvennoye obyedineniye* – 'Leninist' Leningrad Scientific & Production Association), which was one of the Soviet Union's leading avionics houses. It is now known as the Leninets Holding Company.

The work did not proceed beyond the experimental stage. On 18th August 1991 the no longer top secret Mi-26NEF-M was unveiled to the public during an 'open house' at Pushkin near St. Petersburg, LNPO

Leninets's flight test facility. Later the helicopter was converted to a standard Mi-26T, serving with the New Zealand-based airline Heli Harvest as RA-06146.

A prototype was built and tested of the **Mi-26PP** (*postanovshchik pomekh* – ECM aircraft); this was probably '04 Yellow' (c/n 34001212019, f/n 0309) which had large

A Mi-26S sprays decontaminant over a road in the town of Pripyat' in the Chernobyl' nuclear disaster zone.

semi-cylindrical dielectric fairings on the centre fuselage sides. The helicopter remained a one-off and is now a museum exhibit in Togliatti (Samara Region, central Russia).

In 1986, in the wake of the Chernobyl' nuclear disaster, several production Mi-26s were hastily converted for decontamination work in the areas affected by the radioactive fallout. Designated **Mi-26S**, they carried a tank with a special decontaminant fluid in the cargo cabin; a spraybar was fitted ahead of the cargo ramp. Some sources say the decontaminant fluid was in fact a kind of sticky goo meant to keep the dust down and stop it from being carried on the wind.

Perhaps the 'most special-mission version' of The Mi-26 was the one which had a separate designation – **Mi-27**. It was an airborne command post developed in the mid-1980s as a successor to the obsolescent Mi-22. The helicopter's cargo cabin was divided by transverse partitions into a 'war room' for the HQ staff, an equipment bay and a utility compartment. The 'war room' compartment accommodated six staff workstations. The adjoining section provided accommodation for a team operating the mission equipment and maintaining communications; in case of need this section could be used as an extra rest area. The equipment bay housed the radio communications and encoding/decoding suite. The utility section comprised a running water system, a galley, a rest area for two persons and a toilet. To cater for the mission equipment, the standard TA-8V APU was replaced by a more powerful one (probably the TA-6); this was revealed by the different air intake design and the larger exhaust pipe. Two production Mi-26s were converted into Mi-27 prototypes and subjected to testing in Leningrad and Yevpatoriya on the Black Sea. One of them (CCCP-06098) ended its days as a ground instruction airframe at the Khar'kov Institute of the Air Force.

In 1987 the **Mi-26L235 survey helicopter** was converted from a standard Mi-26 at the OKB's Panki facility. Described as 'flying

Seen from another helicopter, a Mi-26S approaches the demolished Unit 4 of the Chernobyl' Power Station.

CCCP-06098, one of the two Mi-27 airborne command posts. Note the extra aerials and the high-set windows of the 'war room'.

laboratory', it was intended for geological prospecting work. No further details have been released. Much later, Rostvertol engineers also developed a project for a similar survey version designated **Mi-26TS** '*Gheolog*' (Geologist). The helicopter, also classed as a 'flying laboratory', was intended for seismic prospecting of oil and gas deposits in offshore areas; it was to deliver to the prospecting site a special platform carried on a sling. The Mi-26TS '*Gheolog*' featured flotation bags in case of ditching, special cargo hatch doors, an SLG-1500 winch, a PSN-6AK inflatable life raft and other necessary devices.

An early project of a medical version designated **Mi-26MS** (*modifitseerovannyy, sanitarnyy* – modified, medical) was demonstrated in model form at the MAKS-93 airshow. Its cargo cabin modules accommodated modular medical equipment, including a surgery compartment. Later, Rostvertol proposed a similar **'flying hospital'/CASEVAC version of the Mi-26TS**. It catered for the delivery of medical personnel, diagnostics, medical treatment of patients on board and their evacuation. The special design features included various functional modules in the cargo cabin to provide intensive therapy en route while retaining the capability to transport equipment for a field hospital (diesel generators and the like) on a sling.

A model of the Mi-26 in a passenger version with rectangular cabin windows – a latter-day Mi-6P – was demonstrated at the MAKS-93; it sported the designation **Mi-26P** (in this case the P stood for *passazheerskiy* – passenger, used attributively). The helicopter was intended to carry 63 passengers over a distance of 750 km (466 miles) at a cruising speed of 250 km/h (155 mph) with a normal AUW of 49,600 kg (109,400 lb). Later, studies

The forward fuselage of the Mi-27, showing the non-standard APU air intake and larger APU exhaust. Note the 'Mi-26' nose titles.

were made at Rostvertol of a 70-seat **'heliliner' version of the Mi-26TS**, as well as of a tourist version with a first-class cabin for 12 passengers and an economy-class cabin for 24 passengers. The designers took into account not only the Russian NLGV-2 airworthiness standards but also the US FAR-29 and European JAR-29 regulations, which made obtaining the Russian and foreign certification seem realistic. To achieve this, a number of complex problems had to be solved, such as ensuring ditchability (a must for overwater operations) and ensuring passenger evacuation within the specified time limit. The associated modifications to the helicopter incurred a weight penalty and cost money (not to mention certification tests, which were particularly expensive). Therefore, to this day the project has not come to fruition.

In 1992 MVZ Mil' drafted a PD project of the **Mi-26M** (*modernizeerovannyy* – upgraded). In order to achieve a performance increase over the baseline Mi-26/Mi-26T the helicopter was to be re-engined with advanced ZMKB Progress (Muravchenko) D-127 turboshafts rated at 14,000 shp; the higher power would probably necessitate a new main gearbox. There were plans to put the Mi-26M into production in 1998.

The cabin of the Mi-27 with the mission equipment operators' workstations.

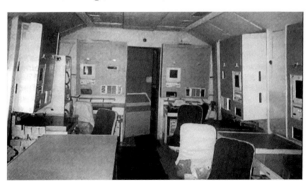

# The Mi-26 in Action

Russian Army Aviation Mi-26s at Mozdok. The type has provided a major airlift capability during both Chechen Wars.

Another apron scene from Mozdok. The Mi-26 in the foreground is a quasi-civil example operated by the Ministry of Interior Troops.

**T**he first military unit to receive the Mi-26 was the Army Aviation's 344th TsBP i PLS in Torzhok where evaluation and aircrew conversion training took place. However, the very first machine delivered to the Centre (c/n 34001212002, f/n 0102) was lost on 26th January 1983 when one of the main rotor blades suffered a spar failure. The crew captained by the Centre's first CO, Maj.-Gen. Nikolay A. Anisimov, was killed in crash. After that the Mi-26s taken on strength by service units underwent tethered tests at Torzhok. After 20-30 minutes of such testing, several faults had to be rectified on each of them.

Not until 1988 did the Mil' OKB and the Rostov plant succeed in curing the teething troubles in the Mi-26's airframe and systems. The work on the helicopter's development was far from completed when Soviet Air Force service units began taking delivery of the type. In 1983 one of the first flight detachments operating the Mi-26 in the USSR was formed within the framework of the KGB's Border Guard Troops. This unit had three helicopters on strength and was included into the 4th OE (*otdel'naya eskadrilya* – Independent Squadron) based at Dushanbe, Tajikistan. That same year the first Mi-26s were delivered to an Army Aviation regiment stationed in the town of Novopolotsk, Belorussian MD.

Mass deliveries of the Mi-26 to the army began in May 1985. In that month two machines were delivered to the 162nd OTBVP (*otdel'nyy trahnsportno-boyevoy vertolyotnyy polk* – Independent Transport and Combat Helicopter Regiment) which was assigned to the Central Asian MD. That same year the 373rd OTBVP stationed at Kyakhta, Buryat ASSR (Trans-Baikalian MD) and the 325th OTBVP stationed at Tselukidze, Georgia (Trans-Caucasian MD) received their first Mi-26s. Later the new helicopters were delivered to the 793rd OTBVP at Telavi, Georgia (Trans-Caucasian MD), the 340th OTBVP at Kalinov in the L'vov Region of western Ukraine (Carpathian MD) and some other units, including the air units of the Ministry

Mi-26 '86 Red' brings supplies to a forward operational location in the North Caucasus, with one of the Russian soldiers securing the perimeter against a possible guerrilla attack in the foreground.

of the Interior. In every regiment the new helicopters equipped two squadrons, each of which had a complement of 12-14 helicopters; the remaining squadrons continued operating Mi-6s or Mi-8s.

Full-scale service tests of the Mi-26 were conducted in the 793rd OTBVP in 1988-89. Col. V. V. Yoodin, a GNIKI VVS test pilot, and Lt.-Col. V. Simakov, Commander of the regiment's 4th Squadron, took part in these tests. In the course of the 13-month evaluation the crews logged 1,414 flying hours; on several occasions the helicopters flew over the Major Caucasus Ridge, climbing to altitudes in excess of 4,500 m (14,800 ft).

The Mi-26 quickly earned the sympathy of airmen. When creating it, the designers had taken into account the complaints voiced with regard to the already obsolescent Mi-6. The pilots liked the excellent view from the flight deck, the high power/weight ratio, good ergonomics, the comfort and life support amenities of the helicopter's pressurised cabin, but it was the reliable and powerful engines that earned the highest praise.

The Mi-26 started its combat career during the Afghan War. Helicopters of this type were not deployed directly in that country, but missions were flown over the northern areas of Afghanistan by machines from the Border Guard Troops' 23rd Regiment stationed in Tajikistan. They fulfilled the typical tasks for heavy helicopters: transportation of various loads, delivery of replenishment troops and evacuation of wounded personnel and the bodies of servicemen killed in action. In the course of such missions the crews had to land on pads situated in the mountains at up to 4,000 m (13,120 ft) above sea level. Unlike the Mi-6, there were no combat losses, but on 18th October 1985 Mi-26 '69 Yellow' (c/n 34001212016, f/n 0306) was lost in an accident. Fuelled with 10 tons (22,045 lb) of kerosene, the helicopter took off from Dushanbe to uplift a load of ammunition at the Moskovskiy border post and deliver it to Kalat-Khuleb in Afghani-

stan, but immediately after take-off from Moskovsky the tail rotor disintegrated. Turning uncontrollably, the helicopter impacted the ground violently and was completely destroyed; the flight engineer was killed, the other members of the crew suffering heavy injuries.

The Mi-26 was put to a major test in 1986 when it took part in damage control operations in the wake of the Chernobyl' nuclear disaster. As early as 2nd May the heavy-lift helicopters arrived from Novopolotsk at the disaster area. To lessen the pernicious influence of radiation, protective lead plating was installed in the cabins. The Mi-26s were used for transportation of various items, and after an appropriate modification they started spraying a special kind of sticky goo intended to immobilise the radioactive dust on the ground and prevent it from being spread by the wind. The plan backfired – during such flights some of the goo stuck to the helicopter's underside, and the rotor downwash kicked up the deadly dust, which also stuck to the machine's belly. The radioactive crust that was thus formed made it virtually impossible to decontaminate the helicopters fully; yet attempts were made to save the costly machines. For example, at

Mi-26 RA-06091 may look civilian and wear Aeroflot titles, but the IRCM flare dispenser housing above the main gear unit reveals this is a quasi-civil MoI Troops example, to say nothing of the BTR-80 APC being unloaded.

Mi-26 '03 Yellow' in MEDEVAC configuration (with appropriate markings) at Kubinka AB in 1991. The code is oddly appropriate, since 03 is the phone number of the ambulance service in Russia!

The cabin of a MEDEVAC-configured Mi-26 with four tiers of stretchers.

Two BMD-2 air-droppable IFVs are loaded into a Mi-26. The helicopter could only transport them, of course – not paradrop them.

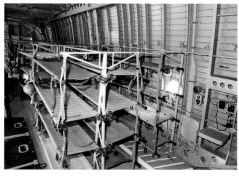

the Rostov plant workers scraped off this crust from the bellies of two Mi-26S 'goo spreaders', using wooden trowels; as it often happened in the Soviet Union, not only were these workers not provided with the necessary means of protection, but much effort was used to make them believe that they were working under normal sanitary condi-

tions. However, such work inevitably had its damaging effect on the workers' health. As for the helicopters… On one of the machines the radiation eventually was reduced to a level exceeding the normal value by a factor of 1.8, and it was pronounced suitable for refurbishment. Another Mi-26S had a radiation level that was ten times the normal value. An attempt was made to decontaminate it once again, this time by military personnel, but these efforts were to no avail, and eventually the machine was struck off charge and relegated to the Rassokha storage and disposal depot.

The Mi-26 rendered valuable assistance during several other complex operations in Chernobyl'. Since service pilots still lacked the necessary experience, such tasks were entrusted to Mil' OKB crews captained by test pilots Gurghen R. Karapetyan and Anatoliy D. Grishchenko who had acquired some skills in transporting loads on an unusually long sling. The first of these operations was to practice the methods of installing a dome-shaped metal cover measuring 19 m (62 ft) in diameter and weighing 15 tons (33,000 lb) over the disabled No.4 reactor to contain the radiation. At first

**Opposite page:**
A Russian Border Guards Mi-26T coded '31 Blue' at Petropavlovsk-Kamchatskiy/Yelizovo airport. The horizontal white stripe is the insignia of the Border Guards Aviation whose badge is also present on the fuselage.

Although the Mi-26 has been in service long enough, the 344th Combat Training & Aircrew Conversion Centre in Torzhok continues to conduct various test and research programmes with the type. Here three Mi-26s are seen at Torzhok in 2011; note the different code colours.

A camouflaged Mi-26 ('07 Yellow') wearing the current-style Russian tricolour stars and 'VVS Rossii' (Russian Air Force) titles seen at Syzran', the seat of a military helicopter pilot school.

**Above:** Mi-26 '01 Yellow' in the latest overall grey colour scheme with tricolour stars and Russian Air Force titles and, as per current practice, a quasi-civil registration (RF-95571).

**Below:** Mi-26 '87 Blue'/RF- (the registration digits have yet to be applied) leads the 2012 Victory Day parade flypast, with two of the four accompanying Mi-8MTV-5-1 helicopters visible here.

**Right:** Here the Mi-26 illustrates its ability to airlift sister ships (suitably lightened, of course).

**Below:** The commercial Mi-26T has been widely used by Aeroflot and its successors since 1986. Here a KS-3575 mobile crane on a ZiL-133GYa chassis is wheeled into Aeroflot Mi-26T CCCP-06118.

**Below right:** An EMERCOM of Russia Mi-26T (RF-32821) lifts a retired Pulkovo Avia Tu-134A at St. Petersburg-Pulkovo on 16th April 2009, transporting it to an EMERCOM training centre in the city's Rybatskoye district for use as a rescue trainer.

Karapetyan, together with an Air Force crew, transported the cover that had been assembled at the Kiev Mechanical Plant named after Oleg K. Antonov (that is, the Antonov OKB) from Kiev-Svyatoshino airfield to the nearby Gostomel' airfield where the Antonov OKB's flight test facility was. There, and later in Chernobyl', some 30 flights were made in which precision installation techniques were evolved, using a mock-up of the reactor. The methods thus developed made it possible to conduct the operation with due regard to the wind direction and to the presence of a very tall chimney located right alongside the destroyed reactor building.

The decision to place the cover directly on the reactor was taken when the test pilots were not on site, and the actual operation was entrusted to service pilots. However, as Grishchenko recalled later, *'they must have been unaware of some limitations known only to us, and the cover was smashed'*. The authorities chose not to manufacture a replacement cover.

When it was decided to restart the Nos. 1-3 reactors of the Chernobyl' power station that had remained intact, the need arose for supplying purified air into the station; for this purpose it was necessary to install special filter units. These were cube-shaped structures measuring 6 x 6 x 6 m (20 x 20 x 20 ft) and weighing 20 tonnes (44,100 lb). Care had to be taken not to descend too low, lest the helicopter should raise clouds of

Mi-26T RA-06273 of Vertical-T in the colourful livery of Uralaviatrans at one of the MAKS airshows.

radioactive dust; again, the work had to be performed with the load on an extra long sling. By then Gurghen R. Karapetyan had been recalled to the OKB, and half of these flights were performed by a crew captained by Anatoliy D. Grishchenko, the remaining 50% falling to the lot of three military crews trained by him. The work at the site of the Chernobyl' disaster proved fatal for Grishchenko: he died of leukaemia in 1990. He was posthumously awarded the Hero of the Russian Federation title.

The Mi-26 saw action in several conflicts that flared up in the Caucasus in the late 1980s/early 1990s. The first of these was the war between Azerbaijan and Armenia for the control over Nagornyy Karabakh which had started during the last years of the Soviet Union's existence. Apart from flights to cater for the needs of the Trans-Caucasian MD's military units, the helicopters delivered humanitarian cargoes for the local population and evacuated refugees. Not infrequently they were fired upon by both belligerents and returned to base with bullet holes.

After the break-up of the USSR a group of the so-called Joint Armed Forces of the CIS (in fact, Russian Army troops) remained

in the conflict area for a while, and the Mi-26s continued their risky flights. On 12th May 1992 Mi-26 '63 Yellow' (c/n 34001212052, f/n 0701) of the 793rd OTBVP was shot down by AA fire near Vaza-shen, Nagornyy Karabakh, during a food supply mission for the Joint Armed Forces of the CIS, killing the crew of five. On 3rd March 1992 another Mi-26 from the same unit ('54 Yellow', c/n 34001212092, f/n 0807) delivered 20 tons (44,090 lb) of flour to Polistan settlement in the Shaumyan District of Nagornyy Karabakh and was expected to evacuate some 50 women and children on the way back. A Mi-24 attack helicopter provided cover for the heavy machine. When the helicopters were already approaching Armenian territory, they were attacked by a Mi-8 without national insignia; it was chased off by the Mi-24. Yet, on short finals the Mi-26 was hit by a shoulder-launched SAM. The helicopter burst into flames and crashed near the village of Seidilyar (Kelbojar Region, Azerbaijan); 12 persons were killed and the remaining occupants suffered injuries.

In 1992 both 'Caucasuian' regiments were withdrawn to the territory of Russia. The

Four Mi-26Ts in the old livery of UTair, Russia's largest commercial helicopter operator.

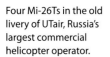

Long-serving Mi-26T RA-06004 displays the striking new livery of UTair. Note the ferry tanks on the right.

Mi-26T RA-06291 in full EMERCOM of Russia colours in 2008. The helicopter is named 'Aleksey Semenkov' as a tribute to an EMERCOM rescue worker who lost his life in the line of duty.

Another EMERCOM of Russia Mi-26T, which is on the government aviation register as RF-32821 'Vasiliy Merkoolov'.

Mi-26T RA-06283 in all-white United Nations colours.

Ukrainian Air Force Mi-26 '54 Black' was operated by the UN Peacekeeping Forces in ex-Yugoslavia in 1995-96.

Another Mi-26T in UN colours (unfortunately wearing neither a registration nor a UN code) rests between missions in company with Mi-8MTV-1 RA-25516 which is also seconded to the UN.

Mi-26T RA-06293 chartered by the International Committee of the Red Cross from Rostvertol-Avia, the manufacturer's flight detachment, for humanitarian operations in Pakistan.

**Opposite page:**
Mi-26T RA-29112 of Vertical-T salvages a US Army MH-47E Chinook downed in Afghanistan in the spring of 2002.

325th OVP, which was stationed at Yegorlyk-skaya AB of the North Caucasian MD after the redeployment, took an active part in both Chechen Wars. Tragically, during the Second Chechen War the Russian Army Aviation suffered its worst combat loss in terms of casualties. On 19th August 2003 a Russian Army Mi-26 coded '89 Red' (c/n 34001212498, f/n 2507) was ambushed by the Chechen bandits while landing at Khankala AB near Groznyy on a troop rotation mission from Mozdok and shot down by a 9K38 *Igla* (Needle; NATO SA-18 *Grouse*) shoulder-launched SAM at 180-200 m (590-650 ft). The helicopter came down in a minefield around the base perimeter and burst into flames. The machine was severely overloaded, with no fewer than 142 (!) passengers, because no flights from Mozdok had been possible in the previous few days due to bad weather. 20 of the passengers and the crew of five captained by Maj. Oleg Batanov survived; the other 127 occupants were killed.

Russia became the largest post-Soviet military operator of the type, which serves with the Air Force, the Border Guards of the Federal Security Service (FSB) and the Ministry of Interior troops. However, not only Russia inherited Mi-26s after the demise of the Soviet Union and the division of its military assets. 28 Mi-26s were taken over by the Ukraine; 24 of them were on the strength of the Army Aviation's 340th OTBVP at Kalinov (or, to use the Ukrainian spelling, Kalyniv) which was reorganised into the 7th Brigade. The Ukrainian Ministry of Emergency Situations took an interest in the Mi-26, and there were plans for transferring several machines to that agency. In the summer 1997 the

Rather weathered Ukrainian Air Force Mi-26 '61 Yellow' undergoes routine maintenance at its home base, Kalinov.

Z2897, the first of four Mi-26s delivered to the Indian Air Force, in the current grey colours.

Mexican Air Force Mi-26 '1901', the first of two delivered.

THE Mi-26 IN ACTION **65**

Ukrainian Ministry of Emergency Situations even demonstrated a Mi-26 in a CASEVAC version at Kiev-Zhulyany airport within the framework of Exercise *Sea Breeze-97*.

The most notable event in the biography of the Ukrainian Mi-26s was their participation in the United Nations peacekeeping mission in former Yugoslavia. Their arrival on the Balkans was preceded by the work of two similar heavy-lifters which were contracted by the UN in early 1995 from the Russian airline Air Troika. Wearing the all-white UN Peace Forces livery, these helicopters delivered supplies for the benefit of the fugitives and transported people, including VIPs attempting to broker a ceasefire. During these flights the choppers were frequently fired upon, which eventually led to a decision to withdraw them from the war zone. As a replacement, the Ukraine sent a pair of military Mi-26s, also painted white for the occasion. The machines were assigned to the 15th OVP and were stationed in the Croatian capital of Zagreb and in the seaside town of Split. Between 29th July 1995 and 14th February 1996 they flew 452 sorties, logging a total of 467 hours; in these flights they transported 2,172 tonnes (4,789,260 lb) of cargo and 2,746 passengers.

By 1999 the designated TBO of all 28 Ukrainian Army Mi-26s had expired. Costly refurbishment was needed to extend the helicopters' service life, but, though the Ukraine had the facilities to do the job, the state budget failed to provide the money and the Mi-26s had to be grounded. Yet, several machines have reportedly been refurbished and returned to service now.

Two more CIS republics inherited the type in 1991. The Belorussian Air Force had about ten Mi-26s based at Kobrin and Machoolishchi AB just south of Minsk, while the Kazakhstan Air Force had close to 20 *Halos*, including two Mi-26TZ tankers, operating from Dzhambul and Pervomaiskoye AB near Almaty.

Production Mi-26Ts started reaching Aeroflot in 1986. The first of them were delivered to the Tyumen' CAD after testing at GosNII GA. At first civil aviation pilots took conversion training directly at the Rostov plant, the Kremenchug Civil Aviation Flying School took over this mission in 1987.

Peruvian Army Aviation Mi-26 EP 725 in a sinister all-black colour scheme.

One of the three Venezuelan Army Mi-26s.

The Equatorial Guinea Air Force operates a single ex-Ukrainian Mi-26.

Apart from that, the following Aeroflot units operated the Mi-26T: the Arkhangel'sk CAD/2nd Arkhangel'sk UAD/68th Flight at Arkhangel'sk-Vas'kovo (now the 2nd Arkhangel'sk Air Enterprise); the Far Eastern CAD/2nd Khabarovsk UAD/249th Flight (now Vostok Airlines); the Komi CAD/Ukhta UAD/302nd Flight (later Komiavia, now called Komiaviatrans); the Krasnoyarsk CAD/2nd Krasnoyarsk UAD; the Tyumen' CAD's Nizhnevartovsk UAD/441st Flight, Nefteyugansk UAD and 1st Tyumen' UAD (later Tyumen'AviaTrans, now called UTair); the Yakutian CAD/Mirnyy UAD (now Alrosa); GosNII GA at Moscow/Sheremet'yevo-1; and VNII PANKh at Krasnodar-Pashkovskiy (now PANKh Avia).

As was the case with its Mi-6 stablemate, the Mi-26's civil applications were primarily concerned with support operations in the areas east of the Ural Mountains rich in oil, diamonds and other natural resources. The Mi-26 proved especially useful for transporting bulky external loads. Many such operations proved to be unique; they became widely known in Russia and abroad, greatly enhancing the helicopter's reputation. Thus, in October 1994 an extremely interesting job was performed during an expedition to Papua New Guinea by a Mi-26T from the Ukhta UAD with a crew captained by A. Fateyev. The airmen were tasked with extracting a Douglas A-20 Boston from a swamp and delivering it to the port of Manang. This bomber, a USAAF 13th Bomb Squadron aircraft, was damaged by Japanese fighters in 1945 and made a belly landing. After restoration the machine was to be donated to the Royal Australian Air Force Museum. Wide plastic straps were wrapped around the Boston's belly and hooked up to the helicopter's sling. When the cable went taut, the weight-measuring device showed a weight of 13 tons (28,700 lb), but when the aircraft was freed from the swamp, the figure was 11 tons (24,225 lb). During this flight the Mi-26 was accompanied by an RAAF Sikorsky S-70 Black Hawk helicopter from which the whole operation was filmed on video.

The Mi-26 was equally efficient in the flying crane role. For example, in December 1995 hundreds of inhabitants of Rostov witnessed the installation of a TV relay tower 30 m (98 ft) tall and weighing 16 tons (35,300 lb) on the roof of the city's Central Telegraph office. It would have taken some two months, with much greater costs, to perform this job with the help of wheeled heavy-duty cranes. In 1997 a Mi-26T belonging to the NPK PANKh enterprise was engaged in the construction of a high-voltage power line in the Krasnodar Territory where it installed 120 power line pylons. In 1998 the helicopter was employed in Germany where it transported an architectural subassembly weighing 11 tons (24,000 lb) and measuring 8 m (26 ft) in diameter from Rostock to Berlin. Several interesting jobs were performed by Mi-26T HL9261 belonging to the South Korean enterprise Samsung Aerospace Ltd.

They include the transportation on a sling of a 15-tonne (33,000 lb) excavator, of a huge statue of Buddha and of a live tree weighing 14 tonnes (30,870 lb) which was to be transplanted to a site 60 km (37 miles) away.

Regrettably, Aeroflot Mi-26s also had their share of accidents. Thus, on 20th March 1990 Mi-26T CCCP-06024 of the Yakutian CAD/Mirnyy UAD crashed near Preobrazhenka settlement (Irkutsk Region/Katanga District) when a hydraulic actuator failed during long line operations, causing loss of longitudinal control. On 18th August 1990, when Mi-26T CCCP-06023 of the Tyumen' CAD/Tyumen' UAD was lifting a slung load near Khanty-Mansiysk airport, the improperly secured cargo broke off. The resulting abrupt stress caused the helicopter to break up in mid-air and crash, again with no survivors.

Russia is now also the primary civil operator of the type, which serves most notably with UTair, Russia's largest commercial helicopter operator. The Mi-26 was also operated by civil airlines in Belarus (Ruby Star) and Moldova (Pecotox Air). Additionally, the type is in service with the civil aid and protection agencies of Russia, Belarus and Kazakhstan; the Mi-26Ts operated by EMERCOM of Russia have done sterling service in the fire-fighting role – both in forestland and in cities.

Like their military sister ships, commercial Mi-26Ts were used a lot for United Nations peacekeeping and humanitarian operations. On 8th December 1992 Rostvertol signed a contract for performing air transport services for the UN Transitional Authority in Cambodia (UNTAC). On 8th July 1993 a similar contract was signed for operations in Somalia (UNOSOM) and Burundi (ONUB – *Opération de l'Organisation de Nations Unies au Burundi*). UTair is an important contractor for the UN in this respect. The airline's Mi-26Ts repainted in all-white UN colours have seen service in Cambodia (UNTAC, 1992-94), East Timor (UNAMET, 2000-2004), Sierra Leone (UNAMSIL, 2000-2013), Liberia (UNMIL, since 2003), the Democratic Republic of Congo (MONUC – *Mission de l'Organisation de Nations Unies en Congo*, since 2003), Sudan (UNMIS, since 2004), Chad (MINUR-CAT – *Mission de Nations Unies au République Centrafricaine et Tchad*, 2008-2011) and South Sudan (UNMISS, since 2011). In a somewhat unlikely twist, civil Mi-26Ts have performed contract work for NATO in Afghanistan. Thus, in the spring of 2002 RA-29112 was famously chartered from Vertical-T, a Russian specialist air work company from Torzhok, to salvage a US Army Boeing MH-47E Chinook that had been downed during Operation *Anaconda* against al-Qaeda and Taliban and which was too heavy to be airlifted by a Sikorsky MH-53E Stallion from the high ground where it sat. In October 2009 a similar operation was performed by RA-06274, also owned by Vertical-T. Unfortunately, such

missions did not always go well; on 14th July 2009 Mi-26T ER-MCV of Pecotox Air was shot down by Taliban guerrillas near Sanghin during a resupply mission, killing the crew composed of Ukrainian nationals.

The Mi-26 has had a measure of success on the export market; both new and second-hand examples were exported to a much wider range of countries compared to the Mi-6. India became the first foreign customer; four helicopters of this type entered service with the Indian Air Force in the early 1980s, although in 2012 the IAF, which held a tender for a new heavy-lift helicopter, rejected the Russian bid of the Mi-26T2 in favour of the CH-47F. The only other military recipient of new Mi-26s is the Army of Venezuela, which bought three. The Algerian Air Force has ordered six, and these may well be Mi-26T2s. The six *Halos* ordered by the Iraqi Air Force were embargoed due to UN sanctions after the Iraqi invasion of Kuwait. Similarly, none of the seven new

Mi-26s built for North Korea were delivered because of sanctions imposed after North Korea withdrew from the Non-Proliferation Treaty and began nuclear testing; later the North Korean Air Force did obtain four second-hand examples. In addition, second-hand Mi-26s were acquired by the air forces of Mexico (two), Malaysia (one), two to the North Korean Air Force, Cambodia (two), Equatorial Guinea (one), Laos (one) and Congo-Kinshasa (one), as well as the Peruvian Army (three). New-build commercial Mi-26Ts have been delivered to South Korea (one) and China (three, with one more on order); additionally, the type has been leased to civil operators in Bulgaria, Belgium, Greece and Papua New Guinea.

At present the Mi-26 is the main helicopter type for airlifting heavy materiel and troops to considerable distances. With new orders coming in to keep the Rostov production line open, the future of the type looks secure.

Mi-26T HL9261 of Samsung Aerospace is pictured here during flying crane operations.

Chinese fire-fighters pose with Mi-26TS B-7802, the first of two bought by Flying Dragon Aviation, in Sichuan Province in 2008.

# The Mi-26 in Detail

The Mi-26 is a military and commercial multi-role heavy helicopter designed for day/night operation in VMC and IMC. The airframe is of all-metal construction and is mostly made of aluminium alloys. The helicopter has a crew of five: captain, co-pilot, navigator, flight engineer and flight technician.

The fuselage is an all-metal semi-monocoque structure built in four sections, each with its own numbering of frames. The detachable *forward fuselage* houses the flight deck and a compartment for cargo attendants. It incorporates a dielectric radome hinged to starboard which encloses the weather radar scanner. The glazing comprises three optically flat windshield panes and four sliding direct vision windows; the latter are bulged for better downward visibility and can be jettisoned in an emergency. The compartment for cargo attendants features two rectangular emergency exits incorporating circular windows. The space beneath the flight deck floor houses avionics and equipment; units of the air conditioning, heating and ventilation system are located on the port side, with the APU bay located symmetrically to starboard. On military Mi-26s,

A cutaway drawing of the Mi-26.

provision is made for protecting the crew with detachable armour plates.

The *centre fuselage* is the main load-bearing part of the airframe; its underside features numerous reinforcement ribs. The cargo cabin (frames 1F-24F) has a floor length of 12.08 m (39 ft 7$\frac{19}{32}$ in) increasing to 15.0 m (49 ft 2$\frac{33}{64}$ in) with the loading ramp included. Maximum cabin height is 3.16 m (10 ft 4$\frac{13}{32}$ in) at frame 17 and 2.95 m (9 ft 8$\frac{6}{64}$ in) at frame 4; the width is 3.2 m (10 ft 5$\frac{6}{64}$ in). Cabin volume is 121 m$^3$ (4,273 cu ft). The rear loading hatch measuring 2.9 x 3.2 m (9 ft 6$\frac{11}{64}$ in x 10 ft 5$\frac{6}{64}$ in) is closed by a cargo ramp and clamshell doors, all of which are hydraulically powered. Each clamshell door incorporates an emergency escape hatch with a window. Up to four vehicle loading ramps can be hooked up to the trailing edge of the cargo ramp.

Personnel access to the interior is via three rectangular airstair doors – one to port at the front and two located symmetrically at the rear; the rear pair are regarded as emergency exits. There are three circular cabin windows to port and four to starboard; the windows open inwards, allowing troopers to use their firearms. An upward-opening dorsal hatch offset to port and accessed via

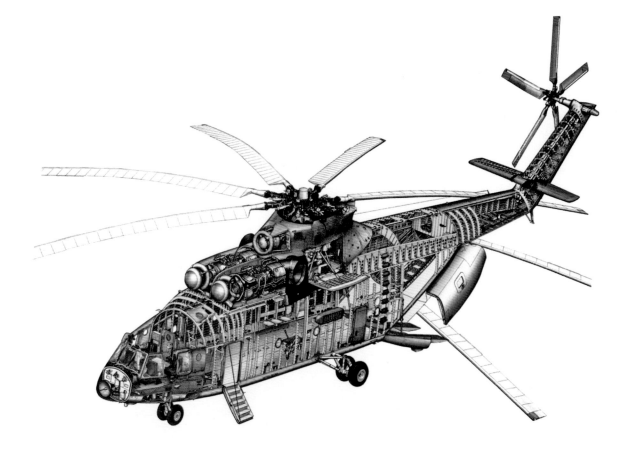

steps on the forward bulkhead of the cabin provides access to the upper surface for maintenance.

Placed dorsally aft of the cabin is the rear compartment (frames 24F-41F) blending into the tailboom. The upper surface of this compartment features a maintenance walkway running further along the top of the tailboom. The ceiling panel (frames 3-24) incorporates attachment fittings for the engines, dust filters, main gearbox mount, cowling panels, control system components and hydraulic unit. The space above the upward-sloping rear portion of the ceiling (frames 18-21) houses the upper container for service fuel tanks (Nos. 9 and 10); these are enclosed by an aerodynamic fairing. On the port side, steps and handrails are mounted externally (frames 23-24) for maintenance access.

The stressed cabin floor can be used for mounting trooper seats or uprights for stretchers (in CASEVAC configuration); it features tie-down facilities for the hardware to be carried and provides place for two winches. There are removable access panels for the installation and servicing of the fuel system and other systems. A large hatch in the centre of the floor closed by doors is provided for the external load suspension system; guardrails are erected around it when the system is in use.

The *tailboom* is joined integrally to the centre fuselage at frame 41; it has a semicircular cross-section with a flat underside. Mounted inside the tailboom are the tail transmission shaft bearings, hydraulics piping and fittings for the attachment of the tail bumper. The tailboom features internal and external walkways for maintenance; it is accessed via a special manhole. A lower panel (frames 7-8) incorporates a hatch for the first of the three TV cameras making up the BTU-1B CCTV system.

The *tail rotor pylon (fin)* consists of front and rear parts joined together along the spar. The forward part houses the intermediate gearbox, the transmission shaft and the final drive tail gearbox, an oil cooler, attachment fittings for the stabiliser and the tail bumper struts, tail rotor control linkages and a built-in ladder. The rear part is a fixed rudder featuring an asymmetrical airfoil to create a side force and off-load the tail rotor in cruise flight; its lower part has a recess for the tail bumper.

The stabilisers have a single-spar structure with a set of ribs, a trailing-edge stringer, fabric skin and attachment fittings. Stabiliser incidence can be adjusted on the ground within a range of +12°/−5°.

The fixed tricycle landing gear has oleonitrogen shock absorbers and twin wheels on each unit. The castoring nose unit has a

The rear end of a Russian Air Force Mi-26 with the port rear entry door and the cargo ramp/clamshell doors open. Note the emergency exits in the clamshell doors.

The cargo cabin of a Mi-26 in troopship configuration with lightweight removable seats on the centreline.

The port engine cowling, main gearbox fairing and main rotor head of a Russian Air Force Mi-26. The object below the engine jetpipe is a fold-away work platform.

semi-levered suspension The strut is attached to centre fuselage frame 1 is fitted with K292/1U non-braking wheels measuring 900 x 200 mm (35.43 x 7.87 in). Each levered-suspension main unit is attached to frames 15 and 17, featuring a KT140D-3 braking wheel outboard and a KT140D-070 non-braking wheel inboard measuring 1,120x450 mm (44x17.7 in). The design of the main landing gear units makes it possible to change the helicopter's ground clearance. A tail bumper is provided to protect the tailboom and tail rotor in a tail-down landing; it consists of a shock absorber, two struts and a tailskid. To facilitate vehicle access to the cargo hatch the tail bumper retracts aft to lie flush with the underside of the tailboom when the cargo doors are opened.

The powerplant consists of two Lotarev (ZMKB Progress) D-136 turboshafts rated at 10,000 shp for take-off, with a contingency rating of 11,400 shp and a maximum sustained power rating of 8,500 shp. The engine has a modular design, five of the nine modules (in the core) being identical to those of the D-36 turbofan. The D-136 is an axial-flow engine with a two-spool core which has a six-stage transonic low-pressure (LP) axial compressor with fixed inlet guide vanes, a seven-stage subsonic high-pressure (HP) axial compressor with variable IGVs and bleed valves at the 3rd and 4th stages, an annular combustion chamber with 24 fuel nozzles and two igniters, and single-stage HP and LP turbines with cooled blades. Located further downstream are a two-stage free turbine with cooled discs and a handed exhaust pipe. An accessory gearbox is mounted on the intermediate case. Starting is by means of an SV-36 air turbine starter (*startyor vozdooshnyy*) using compressed air from the APU, ground supply or cross-feed from the other engine.

EPR at take-off power 18.3, mass flow at take-off power 36 kg/sec (79 lb/sec); turbine temperature at take-off power 1,478°K,

maximum turbine temperature 1,516°K. LP spool speed 10,950 rpm, HP spool speed 14,170 rpm, free turbine speed 8,300 rpm (adjustable by the pilots within ±300 rpm). SFC at take-off power 0.198 kg/hp·hr (0.436 lb/hp·hr), cruise SFC 0.206 kg/hp·hr (0.454 lb/hp·hr). Length overall 3,964 mm (13 ft 0 in), width 1,670 mm (5 ft 5¾ in), height 1,160 mm (3 ft 9⅝ in); dry weight 1,050 kg (2,315 lb).

The D-136 has a self-contained pressure-feed lubrication system, a fuel flow control system maintaining constant engine speed and an electronic engine control system. The powerplant is provided with a system automatically maintaining the pre-set main rotor RPM. In the event of an engine failure the other engine automatically goes to the contingency rating while maintaining a constant main rotor speed (132 rpm).

A Stoopino Machinery Design Bureau TA-8V APU is provided for engine starting, ground power supply and air conditioning. The TA-8V has a single-stage centrifugal compressor, a single-stage peripheral turbine, a 12-kW GS-12TO DC starter/generator and a GT40PCh6 AC generator. Dimensions, 1.368 x 0.701 x 0.717 m (4 ft 5⅞ in x 2 ft 3¹⁹⁄₃₂ in x 2 ft 4¹⁵⁄₆₄ in), dry weight with generator 216 kg (476 lb). Bleed air pressure 3.3 bars (47 psi), delivery rate 0.75 kg/sec (1.65 lb/sec), equivalent power 107 kW, fuel consumption 145 kg/h (320 lb/h). The APU can be started at altitudes up to 5,000 m (16,400 ft).

The engines, together with the main gearbox and the cooling fan assembly, are enclosed by a large fairing incorporating multi-section cowlings which fold down to act as work platforms during maintenance, as well as longitudinal and transverse firewalls made of OT4-0 titanium alloy. The air intakes feature vortex-type dust/debris extractors with an extraction rate of 70-75%.

Engine torque is fed via overrunning clutches into the VR-26 main gearbox which reduces the engine transmission shafts' rotation speed and conveys torque to the main rotor, tail rotor drive shaft and the fan serving the engine oil coolers and main gearbox oil cooler. It has a modular three-stage design; length 2.5 m (8 ft 2⅜ in), width 1.95 m (6 ft 5 in), height 3.02 m (9 ft 11 in), dry weight 3,640 kg (8,026 lb). The main gearbox mounts a rotor brake which also serves as a parking brake for the power train. The main gearbox has a pressure lubrication system using B-3V grade oil, with a capacity of 250 litres (55 Imp gal). The oil is cooled in four air/oil heat exchangers.

The space between the handed canted sections of the exhaust pipes is occupied by the cooling fan driven off the main gearbox; its air intake and air duct are located ahead of the main rotor head. The fan serves the oil coolers of the engines, the main gearbox and the hydraulic system, as well as the air/air heat exchanger of the AK-50T1 air compressor; it cools the engines' free turbine casings and the rotor speed governor.

The tail shaft housed inside the tailboom transmits torque from the main gearbox to the tail rotor via the PR 90-1515-000 intermediate tail gearbox (*prome**zhoo**tochnyy re**dook**tor*) and the KhR 90-1515-000 final drive tail gearbox (*khvosto**voy** re**dook**tor*). The intermediate gearbox located at the base of the tail rotor pylon serves for changing the direction of the tail shaft axis by 44°. The final drive gearbox turns the shaft through 90° to starboard; it incorporates the tail rotor pitch control mechanism.

The *main rotor* turning clockwise when seen from above has eight hinged blades of constant 0.835-m (34-in) chord having an airfoil with a thickness/chord ratio of 12% at the shank and 9% at the tip. Each blade has a steel spar/leading-edge section, 26 glass-fibre trailing-edge pockets with a paper filler, a shank fairing and a tip fairing; pockets Nos. 17-19 are fitted with balance tabs used for adjusting the main rotor. The blades feature a compressed-air spar failure warning system. The blade tip speed is 220 m/sec (722 ft/sec).

The main rotor head manufactured of VTZ-1 grade titanium features feathering, flapping and drag hinges, as well as centrifugal blade droop stops. The flapping and drag hinges are separated from each other, the flapping hinges being turned 6°58'.

The five-blade pusher-type *tail rotor* is mounted on the starboard side of the fin, turning anti-clockwise when seen from the hub so that the forward blades go against the main rotor downwash, increasing the relative speed. The tail rotor head has separate flapping and feathering hinges. The blades have constant 0.47-m (18½ in) chord and a NACA-230M airfoil; each blade has a glassfibre spar, an integral trailing-edge section and a tip fairing.

The Mi-26 has full powered dual controls with mechanical linkage. The control system features two spring-loading devices with EMT-2MP electromagnetic brakes, two KAU-140 combined actuators and the swashplate mounted on the main gearbox. Pitch and roll control is effected with the help of the swashplate; directional control is effected by changing the amount of tail rotor thrust. The combined control units are incorporated into the control system on the basis of a differential layout and function independently. They double as hydraulic actuators and as servos of the VUAP-1 Srs 2 autopilot.

The fuel system comprises ten bag-type tanks, two boost pumps, four transfer pumps, two units of jet pumps, shut-off valves, float valves and piping. The tanks are made of 203B grade kerosene-resistant rubber and have an external protective layer of 11KShZOO grade rubberised fabric. The Nos. 4, 5, 9 and 10 tanks have a self-sealing layer of R-29 grade foam rubber protecting against damage by small-arms fire. All tanks are housed in special containers forming an integral part of the fuselage structure. Provision is made for two or four long-range tanks of welded aluminium alloy construction in the cargo cabin. The total fuel capacity is 26,662 litres (5,866 Imp gal), including 9,650 litres (2,123 Imp gal) in the eight main tanks, 2,246 litres (494 Imp gal) in the two service tanks and up to 14,736 litres (3,242 Imp gal) in the long-range tanks.

The Mi-26 has three hydraulic systems. The *main* and *back-up systems* cater for the KAU-140 combined actuators of the control system; the backup system also serves for

The nose landing gear unit.

The port main landing gear unit of a Russian Air Force Mi-26. The port IRCM flare launcher housing is visible above it.

The tail rotor.

checking the flight controls on the ground with the engines shut down when no ground hydraulic power unit is available. In flight the *auxiliary system* works the hydraulic damper in the yaw control circuit, the upper lock of the external load suspension system, enables emergency closing of the cooling fan's guide vanes, operates the retractable tail bumper, the mainwheel brakes and the helicopter weight measuring system. AMG-10 hydraulic fluid is used throughout. The tank of the main hydraulic system holds 41 litres (9.02 Imp gal); the back-up and auxiliary systems have a common 53-litre (11.66 Imp gal) tank. The nominal pressure of 160-220 kg/cm² (2,285-3,142 psi) is pro-

## ■ **Mi-26** SPECIFICATIONS

| | |
|---|---|
| Length, rotors turning | 40.025 m (131 ft 3²⁵⁄₃₂ in) |
| Fuselage length | 33.745 m (110 ft 8³⁵⁄₆₄ in) |
| Height on ground | |
| at main rotor head | 8.145 m (26 ft 8⁴⁵⁄₆₄ in) |
| Main rotor disc area | 804.25 m² (8,656 sq ft) |
| Main rotor diameter | 32 m (104 ft 11 in) |
| Tail rotor diameter | 7.61 m (24 ft 11³⁹⁄₆₄ in) |
| Landing gear track | 5.0 m (16 ft 4⁵⁄₆₄ in) |
| Landing gear wheelbase | 8.95 m (29 ft 4²³⁄₆₄ in) |
| Empty weight | 28,150 kg (62,070 lb)* |
| Take-off weight: | |
| normal | 49,500 kg (109,150 lb) |
| maximum | 56,000 kg (123,480 lb) |
| Payload: | |
| normal internal | 15,000 kg (33,075 lb) |
| maximum internal | 20,000 kg (44,100 lb) |
| external | 20,000 kg (44,100 lb) |
| Speed: | |
| maximum | 295 km/h (183 mph) |
| cruising | 255 km/h (158 mph) |
| Hovering ceiling: | |
| out of ground effect | 1,800 m (5,900 ft) |
| in ground effect | 2,900 m (9,510 ft) |
| Service ceiling | 4,600 m (15,090 ft) |
| Operational range: | |
| with maximum load | 475 km (295 miles) |
| with maximum fuel | 800 km (496 miles) |
| Ferry range | |
| with four extra tanks | 1,920 km (1,190 miles) |

* Also stated as 28,200 kg (62,170 lb) or 28,600 kg (63,050 lb)

vided by four NP-92A plunger-type pumps driven off the main gearbox. With the engines shut down, hydraulic pressure is provided by two NS46-2 pump units in the main and the backup systems and an NP01/1 manually operated pump in the auxiliary system.

The pneumatic system works the main-wheel brakes, the perimeter seals of the flight deck blister windows and emergency exits in the cargo attendants' compartment for protection against nuclear, biological and chemical (NBC) contaminants. It also feeds the windshield washer system. The AK-50T1 Srs 3 engine-driven compressor provides the nominal pressure of 40-50 kg/cm² (571-714 psi) and charges two UBSh-4 air bottles with a total capacity of 8 litres (1.76 Imp gal).

The electric system comprises primary, secondary and auxiliary systems. *Primary* 200 V/400 Hz and 115 V/400 Hz three-phase AC power is supplied by two GT-90S46 engine-driven generators (*ghen-erah*tor *tryokhfahz*nyy) with a capacity of 120 kVA; a PO-750A single-phase AC converter serves as an emergency source. The three *secondary systems* comprise 36 V/400 Hz single- and three-phase AC systems with a PT-200P three-phase AC converter as an emergency source. The *auxiliary system* includes a GT-40P46 AC generator driven by the APU. AC/DC ground power receptacles are provided on the port side of the nose. The electric system caters for the avionics, lighting equipment and cargo handling equipment. The lighting equipment comprises interior and exterior lighting; the latter includes navigation lights, two anti-collision beacons (under the centre fuselage and on the tailboom), main rotor blade tip lights, and formation lights used for night landing assault operations.

The engine air intakes, rotor blades, flight deck windshields, pitot heads and static ports are electrically de-iced. The fire suppression system features type 2-16-5 fire extinguishers for fighting fires in the engine bays and the APU bay.

The Mi-26's *flight and navigation system* comprises a 7A813 weather radar, ARK-22 and ARK-UD automatic direction finders, a **Vey**er-M (Fan) short-range radio navigation system, a DISS-32-90 Doppler speed and drift sensor, an RV-A036 radio altimeter, DPSM-1 airspeed sensors, DV-15MV altitude sensors, an air data system (four pitot heads and six static ports), thermometers, the port and starboard MGV-1 SUV vertical gyros, a KI-13K compass, a **Greben'**-2 compass system (the name may translate as 'haircomb' – or as 'ridge') and a PKV-26-1 flight control system featuring a VUAP-1 Srs 2 autopilot.

The *communications suite* comprises an R-863' command link radio, a Yadro-1I-1 communications radio, an R-861 emergency and rescue radio and an SPU-8 intercom. An RI-65 automatic audio warning system (*reche***voy** *info***mah**tor – voice annunciator) informs the crew of critical failures and dan-

The flight deck of an early-production Mi-26T, with the flight engineer's and radio operator's workstations in the foreground. The blue spherical objects are oxygen bottles.

gerous flight modes. The *IFF system* features an SRO-2M Khrom or SRO-1P *Parol'*-2D (Password; *izdeliye* 62-01) IFF transponder; an SO-69 air traffic control transponder transmits the aircraft's registration, speed and altitude for presentation on ATC radar displays and may operate in 'Mayday' mode. The *electronic support measures (ESM) equipment* comprises an L006 *Beryoza* (Birch) radar homing and warning system alerting the crew that the helicopter is being 'painted' by enemy radars. On military Mi-26s, two ASO-2V IRCM flare dispensers with 46 IPP-26 magnesium flares are mounted in lateral fairings near the engine jetpipes for protection against heat-seeking missiles.

Other special equipment includes a BTU-15 closed-circuit TV system (*bortovaya televizionnaya oostanovka* – on-board TV installation) with three KT-45 TV cameras and a VK-175 TV display for checking the underslung load's condition. A DP-ZA-1 roentgenometer is provided for radiation reconnaissance in NBC-contaminated areas. The helicopter features a BUR-1-2B (Tester-UZ) FDR and an MS-61B cockpit voice recorder.

The cabin equipment comprises collapsible/removable seats for 82 fully equipped troops; optional medical equipment for the transportation of 60 stretcher cases; and cargo handling equipment comprising two LG-1500 electric winches, two overhead cranes, cargo tie-down cleats, roller conveyers, hooks and a system for the carriage of slung loads. The latter system comprises the external suspension hook with a device for measuring the load's weight, an LG-1500 winch, the BTU-1B CCTV system, slings and cables. The external suspension system is hydraulically and electrically controlled; the control devices ensure the disengagement of the load for operational purposes and its jettisoning in an emergency.

The updated flight deck of Mi-26T RA-06255.

# The Modeller's Corner

## 1:72nd scale

As promised, **Sanger** (aka **Sanger-Contrail**) followed up on the Mi-6 with a vacuform and white metal kit of the Mi-26. The kit consists

of 108 parts, including 66 white metal parts. The fuselage is again moulded in two halves integrally with the tailboom and shows some inaccuracies in the contours of the lower fuselage and the nose section. Decals are provided for Mi-26T RA-29109 in temporary EMERCOM of Russia colours.

As for injection moulded kits, the first 1:72nd scale kit of the *Halo* was issued in 2006 (not in the 1990s, as some sources claim) by the Russian company **Yoozhnyy Front**, or **South Front** (Ref. No.72001). The company is based in Rostov-on-Don in southern Russia (which explains the name) – the birthplace of the real Mi-26, so one might expect the model to be accurate. And so it is – the dimensions and outlines almost exactly match the scale plans from the Mi-26 monographic feature in *Aviatsiya i Vremya* No.6-2000.

The large box contains no fewer than 24 sprues (22 moulded in a soft light grey plastic and two clear sprues) with a total of 234 parts. The first page of the detailed Russian/English assembly instruction booklet resembles that of the actual Mi-26 structural manual. The painting instructions give Akan enamel numbers and US Federal Standard codes as a painting guide. The very comprehensive decal sheet features all maintenance stencils and lets you build any of three camouflaged Soviet/Russian Air Force Mi-26s *sans suffixe* coded '68 Yellow' (Chernobyl' nuclear disaster control), '90 Red' (First Chechen War) or '69 Yellow' (Second Chechen War), Mi-26T CCCP-29109 in Aeroflot colours or all-white Mi-26T RA-06181/UN-835 seconded to the United Nations Mission in Congo (MONUC).

**Top:** The box top of the South Front kit showing a Mi-26 flying over the Chernobyl' nuclear power station.

**Above and right:** The South Front Mi-26 built by a modeller with the internet alias Helifan.

The fuselage is split into the forward section, the centre section and the tailboom/ tail rotor pylon together with the rear end of the cabin, all in left and right halves. The clamshell cargo doors and cargo ramp are separate parts. The fuselage components have a smooth surface finish and finely engraved panel lines, with very little flash, and the flight deck transparencies are very clear (except the lateral blister windows, which could use some polishing), but... This is a 'short run' kit; as a result, the major parts' geometry is inconsistent. Some kit builders report the South Front Mi-26 went together well, while others provide proof that the major parts are a poor fit, with warped components showing mismatches of up to 1 mm and requiring a lot of filling (especially the forward/centre fuselage joint. Also, unlike the detailed flight deck, the cavernous cargo cabin is starkly empty – even the fuselage frames are not reproduced on the cabin walls (albeit the formers on the inside of the clamshell doors are reproduced). In a nutshell, the finished model looks impressive as hell but takes a lot of effort to build and has room for improvement.

In 2008 another Russian kit manufacturer, **Zvezda** (Star), released its own 1:72nd scale version of the Mi-26 (Ref. No.7270). It should be noted that Zvezda is a much larger manufacturer and uses the conventional

high-pressure injection moulding technology, with an accordingly better surface finish; the Mi-26 is no exception.

The flip-top box, whose artwork changed subtly in the autumn of 2010, contains six sprues moulded in light grey polystyrene and one clear sprue, with a total of 234 parts. The manufacturer has taken pains to prevent damage to the parts – the opaque sprues are packed in individual polyethylene bags (!), while the clear parts are in a small cardboard box preventing scratches – and it's just as well because they are very delicate. The breakdown of the kit is rather different from South Front's Mi-26 thanks to

**Above:** The box top of the Zvezda Mi-26 kit as it looked in January 2012; the font and placement of the inscriptions changed by September 2012 but the artwork remained the same.

**Left:** The Zvezda Mi-26 built by Pavel Sadovoy to represent a Ukrainian Air Force/340th OTBVP machine (c/n 34001212153) operated in 1994. The model was built out of the box with various alterations to the flight deck and the cabin. Scratchbuilt aerials, pitots, windshield wipers, handles, steps and railings were added, the walkway on the tailboom was extended rearward, hydraulic lines were added and the main gear units were 'doctored' to emulate the oleo compression typical of a loaded helicopter. Blade tip lights and anti-collision lights were added. The model was painted with Gunze Sangyo acrylic paints, the insignia and tactical code being sprayed on; Fan Color water soluble paint, Tamiya pigments and pastel colours were used for weathering. The top coat was Gunze Sangyo satin varnish on the forward fuselage and Gunze Sangyo matt varnish elsewhere to emulate the much smaller degree of weathering where the paintwork is under wraps when the chopper is parked.

The Zvezda Mi-26 built as an EMERCOM of Russia Mi-26T by a modeller with the internet alias wbdesign from Orenburg, Russia. Minor alterations were made to the flight deck and the cargo cabin interior (in the latter case the fuselage frames were made bolder by gluing on strips of plastic card and tip-up seats were added). Blade leading-edge sheaths made of aluminium foil and hydraulic piping on the main rotor head and main gear units were added, as were the maintenance steps on the port side, external handles, aerials and anti-collision lights; the excessively thick pitots were 'doctored' a little to bring them to scale, using wire. The model was painted with Zvezda Super enamels; the orange colour of the EMERCOM stripes was sprayed on and the blue parts were added as decals.

The Zvezda Mi-26 built by Anatoliy Lysenko aka Rowdy to represent a Russian Air Force/344th TsBP i PLS machine used for CASEVAC duties. Various small exterior details (pitots, aerials, steps and so on) were added. The model was painted with Tamiya and Gunze Sangyo acrylic paints, with post-shading, and finished off with Begemot decals from the No.72-031 set.

The Zvezda Mi-26 built by a modeller with the internet alias Kaspiy from Aktau, Kazakhstan. The model was painted with Vika automotive enamel.

the different technology – the fuselage is moulded in two halves integrally with the tailboom, facilitating assembly, while the tail rotor pylon (also in two halves) and the forward fuselage roof are separate parts. An important advantage over the South Front kit is the detailed cabin interior with inte-

grally moulded fuselage frames and the option of modelling the three entry doors in the open position; also, the rotor hubs are very detailed and the main rotor blades are pre-drooped for added realism. The fuselage halves are properly thin, which is good for scale but makes them prone to warping;

also, the engraved panel lines are somewhat on the shallow side, in the opinion of some reviewers. Generally the model matches the scale plans well, but there have been reports that the flight deck windows are out of scale, being too large. The detailed instruction sheet is in Russian, English (though at times it seems to be more like 'Runglish'), Italian, German, French and Spanish; Zvezda and Model Master enamel numbers are given as a painting guide. Optional parts and the decal sheet, which features the instrument panels and some of the maintenance stencils, let you build a Russian Federal Border Guards Mi-26 *sans suffixe* ('99 Yellow') deployed to Tajikistan in 1993 or the above-mentioned Mi-26T RA-06181/UN-835. A major shortcoming is that Zvezda has not manage to tackle the tricky issue of applying the star insignia to the ribbed underside of the fuselage and therefore chose to omit this star altogether... Begemot Decals to the rescue!

It is not uncommon for Russian kit manufacturers to offer reboxed versions of kits by western manufacturers (and Zvezda is a case in point), but occasionally the trend is

reversed. In 2009 **Revell** hit the market with a repackaged version of the Zvezda Mi-26 kit (Ref. No.04645). This has different box art and different decals to build a Russian Air Force Mi-26 in standard camouflage ('90 Red') or a red-starred Belorussian Air Force machine with a huge sharkmouth ('56 Red').

The box top of the Zvezda Mi-26 kit repackaged by Revell.

# 1:144th scale

Here we have the same 'cast of characters' as in the Mi-6 section. Again, **Air Craft Models** was probably the first to release a 1:144th scale kit of the Mi-26 – a vacuform/white metal kit (Ref. No.412). Next, in 2010 **LEM Models** issued a resin/white metal kit of the Mi-26. The kit consists of 43 parts and the fuselage breakdown is similar to that of the Mi-6 kit. The decal sheet lets you build a Soviet/Russian Air Force Mi-26 *sans suffixe* ('50 Yellow' or '99 Yellow') or Mi-26T RA-06181/UN-835 (this particular helicopter in MONUC colours seems to be a perennial favourite with kit manufacturers).

In 2012 **Eastern Express/Vostochnyy Ekspress** released two 'short run' kits – the military Mi-26 *sans suffixe* and the commercial Mi-26T. Both are labelled 'Heavy Multi-Purpose Helicopter Mi-26' and differ only in the decals – traditionally supplied by Begemot Decals. The former kit (Ref. No.14502) lets you build any of three Soviet/Russian Air Force machines ('04 Blue', '07 Yellow' and '92 Yellow'), the star insignia featuring an optional blue outline for reproducing the current Russian Air Force insignia as appropriate, or two EMERCOM of Russia machines registered RF-31351 and RF-32821. The other (Ref. No.14503) gives a choice of the first prototype Mi-26 (CCCP-06181) in Aeroflot colours, Mi-26T RA-06082 in the predominantly white livery of UTair and, in some versions of the decal sheet, stars and codes for Soviet Air Force '04 Blue' for good measure, in case you become military-minded in the course of the project.

The kit comprises 85 parts on four sprues moulded in light grey plastic and one clear sprue (the latter is of rather poor quality). The fuselage comes in two halves with an integrally moulded tailboom; the centre fuselage underside, the underside of the tailboom and the tail rotor pylon (in two halves) are moulded separately. This time there are no provisions for leaving the cargo doors open; the cabin windows are properly reproduced (no need to drill them out), but the decal sheet still includes dark shapes for all the windows as an alternative. The flight deck interior is *very* basic – but then, not much will be visible in this scale. The parts fit is rather poor; small items like aerials, pitots or even the APU exhaust are not included.

The box top of the Eastern Express Mi-26 kit.

**Above and right:** The Eastern Express Mi-26T built 'out of the box' by Marco Coldewey from Germany. The fuselage halves were seriously warped at the bottom, requiring holes to be drilled and bits of wire to be inserted to prise them apart as the floor was glued into place; a lot of filler was required around the flight deck transparency. The stock tail bumper, which was substandard, was replaced by a scratchbuilt version; windshield wipers and pitots have been added, but not the guide rails for the sliding side windows. Note that the tail rotor has been glued incorrectly, turning clockwise when seen from the hub (it should be anti-clockwise).

**Above right:** The box top of the Eastern Express Mi-26T kit.

## AFTERMARKET ITEMS

There is an adequate selection of aftermarket items for those who are not content with an 'out-of-the-box' *Halo* – albeit in 1:72nd scale only (none are available for the 1:144th scale kits). In 2010 the Czech company **Eduard Models** released a couple of photo-etched parts sets for the Zvezda/Revell kit (though they can probably be used for improving other kits as well). The first of these (Ref. No.72507) is an exterior parts set which includes the tailboom walkway, the flight deck blister window guide rails, rotor hub parts and so on. The other (Ref. No.73356) is an interior parts set comprising two PE frets – one for the flight deck and one for the cargo cabin. The former fret, which also has a separate reference number (SS356), features pre-painted instrument panels and seat belts both for the crew seats and for the jump seats at the back; the instrument panels are self-adhesive – a particularly neat feature. The other fret has the innermost formers for the clamshell cargo doors (with lightening holes), new boarding steps and lock actuating linkages for the entry doors, the access ladder for the dorsal escape/maintenance hatch at the front of the cabin, and access steps for the inside of the tailboom attached to the inside of the clamshell doors. Both sets

have been reissued by the Russian company **EdModels** as Ref. Nos. ERU72003 and ERU72004 respectively (albeit some sources report the EdModels version appeared in 2008). The Polish accessories supplier **Part** has also issued an exterior/interior parts set for the South Front and Zvezda/Revell kits (Ref. No.S72-252) comprising two PE frets and a printed clear sheet with the instrument panels. Finally, a company called **Fairy Hobby** offers a set of weighted wheels cast in resin for the South Front and Zvezda/Revell kits (Ref. No.FH72004).

Decals are not a problem either – in addition to the stock decals for the South Front and Eastern Express kits, **Begemot Decals** offers a magnificent five-sheet set of 1:72nd scale decals for the *Halo* (Ref. No.72-031). This gives you a choice of 39 colour schemes of civil, paramilitary and military Mi-26s from the Soviet Union, Russia, the Ukraine, India, Mexico, Belgium, the Democratic Republic of Congo, South Korea, Belarus, Peru, Venezuela and China. Notably, the set includes a version of the red star insignia 'doctored' for applying correctly to the fuselage underside with its many stiffening ribs. Various maintenance stencils are provided for the cabin interior, and the painting instructions are very detailed.

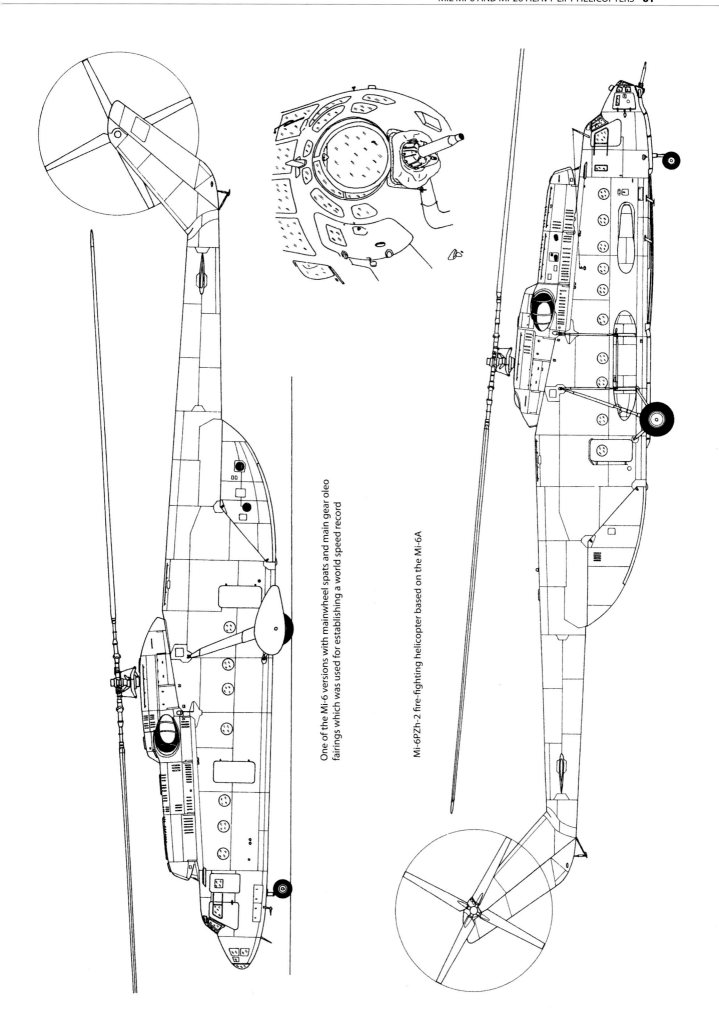

One of the Mi-6 versions with mainwheel spats and main gear oleo fairings which was used for establishing a world speed record

Mi-6PZh-2 fire-fighting helicopter based on the Mi-6A

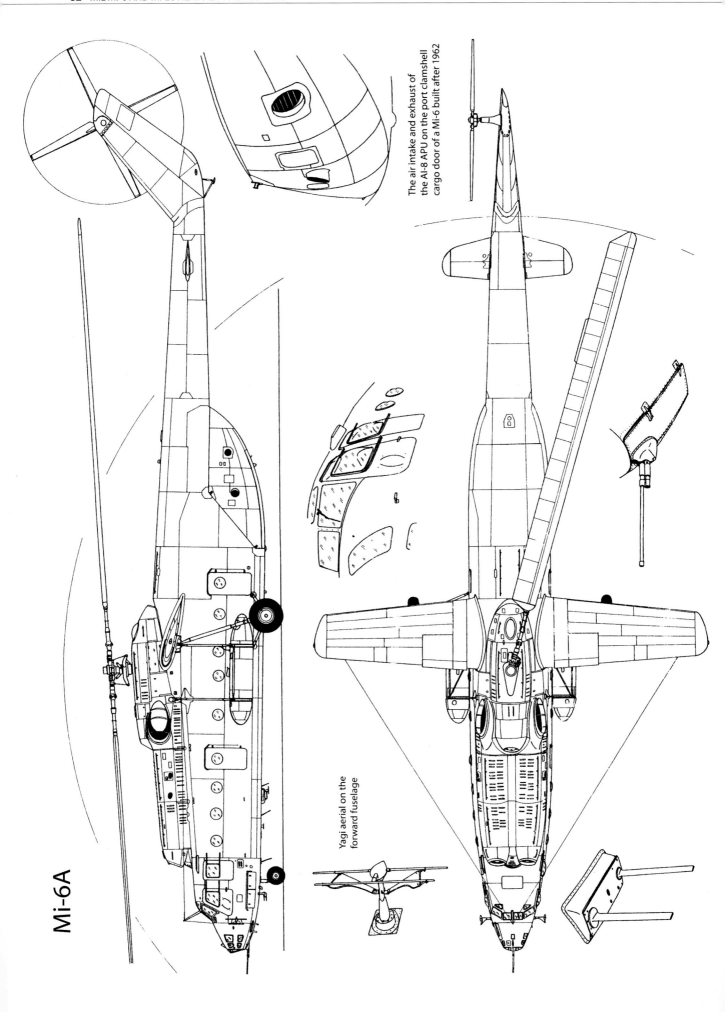

The air intake and exhaust of
the AI-8 APU on the port clamshell
cargo door of a Mi-6 built after 1962

Yagi aerial on the
forward fuselage

Mi-6A

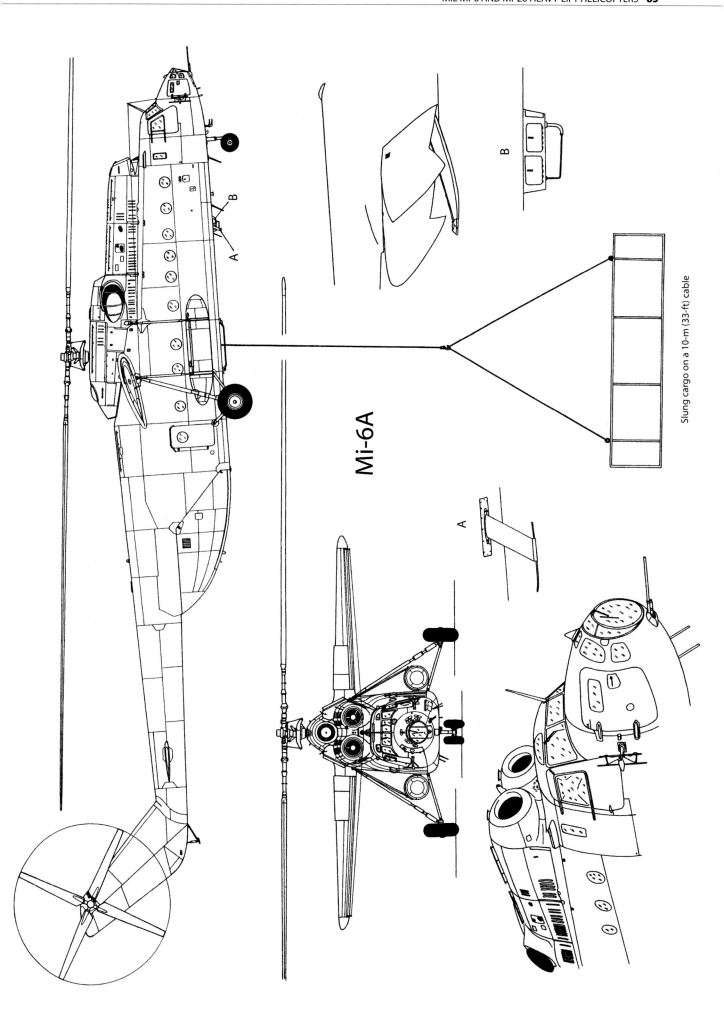

Mi-6A

Slung cargo on a 10-m (33-ft) cable

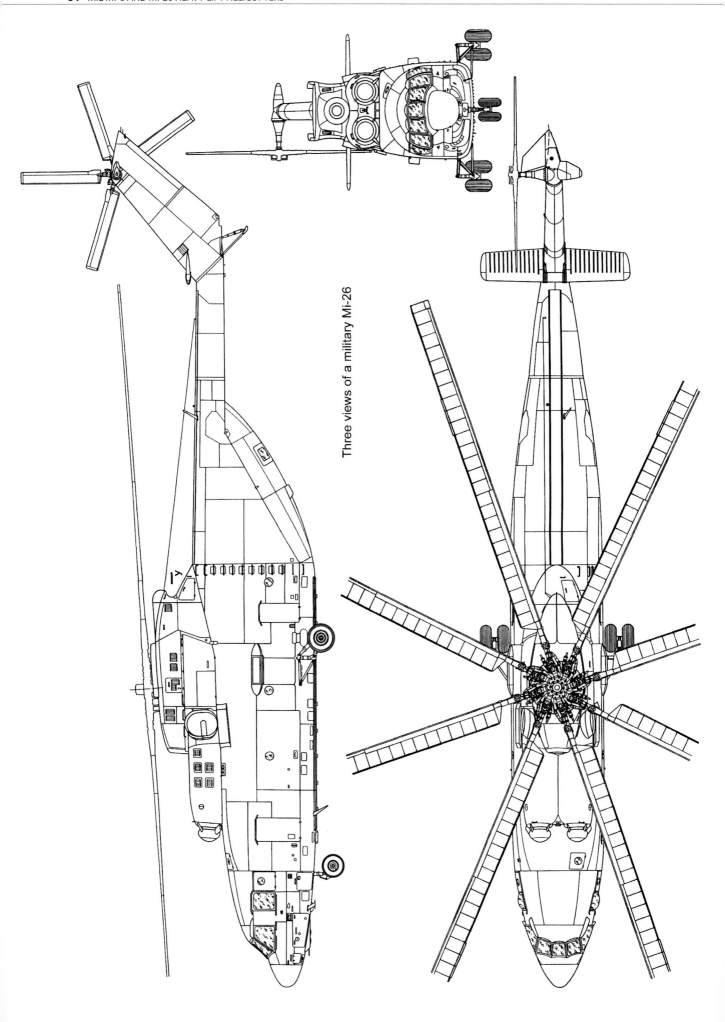

Three views of a military Mi-26

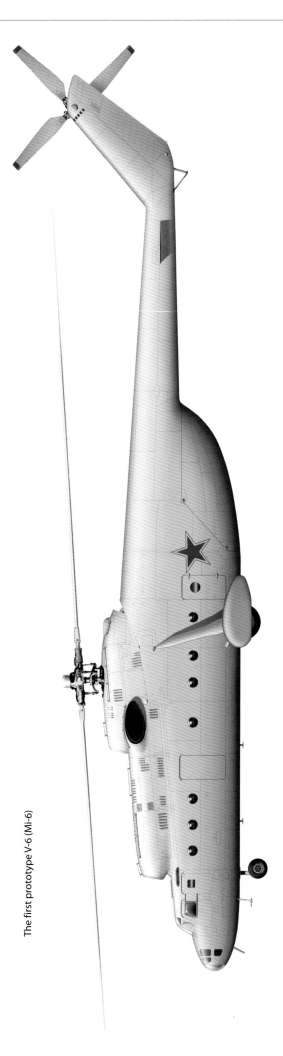

The first prototype V-6 (Mi-6)

An early-production Moscow-built Mi-6 (c/n 1030302V)

I030302B

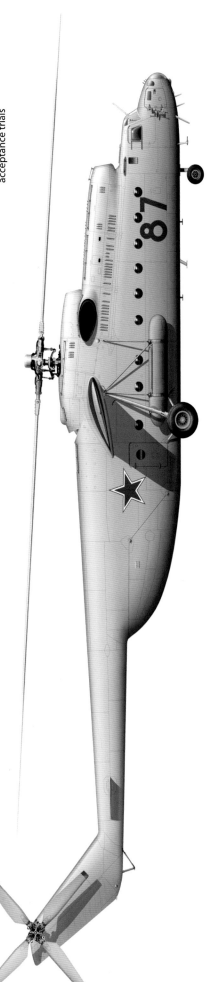

Soviet Air Force Mi-6 '87 Red' which participated in the type's state acceptance trials

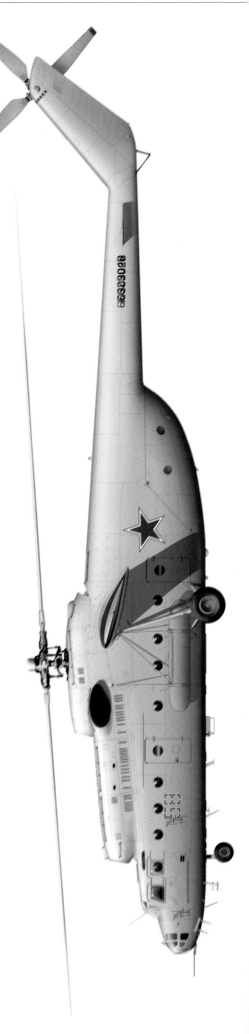

'58 Red' (c/n 6682904V), a late production standard Rostov-built Mi-6

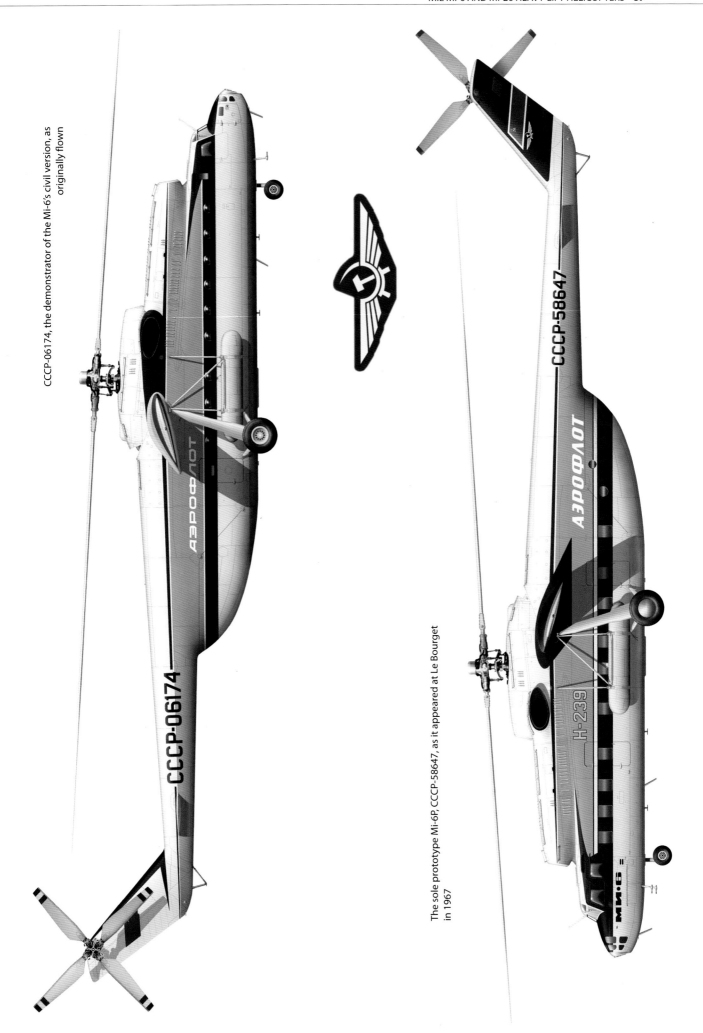

CCCP-06174, the demonstrator of the Mi-6's civil version, as originally flown

The sole prototype Mi-6P, CCCP-58647, as it appeared at Le Bourget in 1967

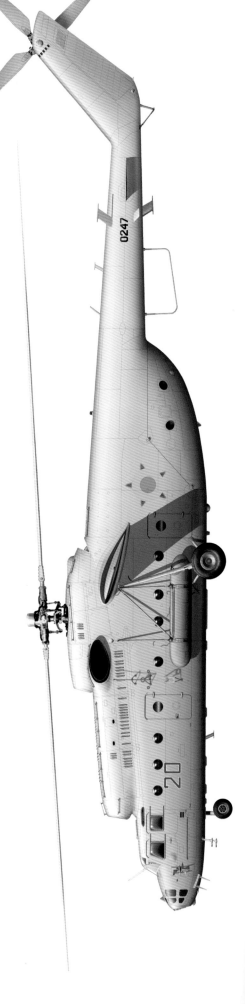

Mi-6PZh-2 '41 Yellow' (c/n 9683901V)

Ukrainian Air Force Mi-6VKP '22 Blue' (c/n 0247)

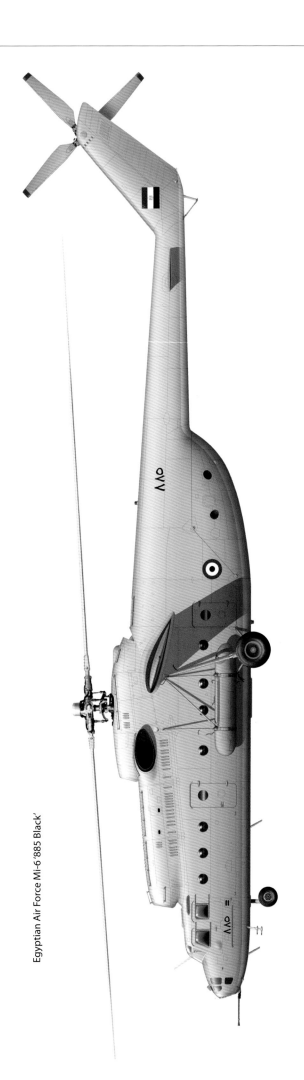

Egyptian Air Force Mi-6 '885 Black'

Indonesian Air Force Mi-6 H-275; the serial is applied in the late 'split' style

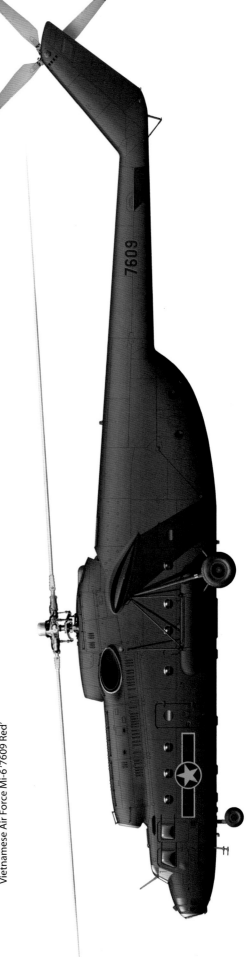

Polish Air Force Mi-6A '671 White'

Vietnamese Air Force Mi-6 '7609 Red'

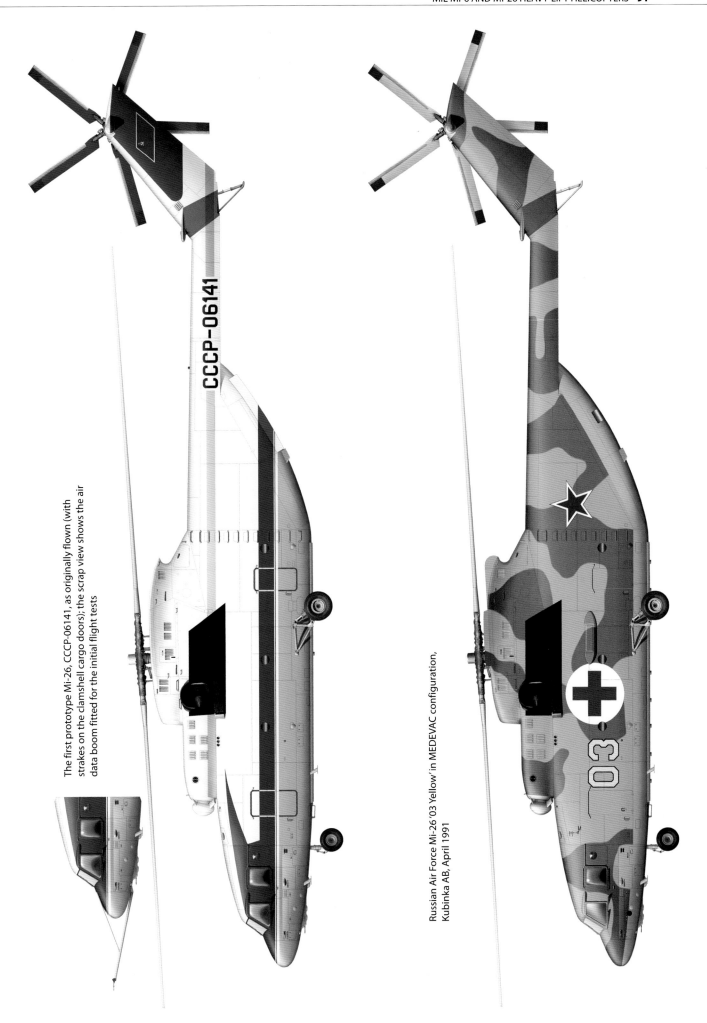

The first prototype Mi-26, CCCP-06141, as originally flown (with strakes on the clamshell cargo doors); the scrap view shows the air data boom fitted for the initial flight tests

CCCP-06141

Russian Air Force Mi-26 '03 Yellow' in MEDEVAC configuration, Kubinka AB, April 1991

Russian Federal Border Guards Aviation Mi-26 '31 Blue'

Russian Air Force Mi-26 '03 Blue'

Ukrainian Air Force Mi-26 '64 Black' seconded to the United Nations
Peace Force in former Yugoslavia, 1994

UNITED NATIONS

64

U·N

МИ-26

Mi-26T RA-06285 operated by the Moscow Aviation Centre, an
organisation affiliated with EMERCOM of Russia

RA-06285

МОСКОВСКИЙ АВИАЦИОННЫЙ ЦЕНТР

ВВС РОССИИ

ВВС РОССИИ

Russian Air Force Mi-26 '91 Red' with new-style tricolour star insignia and 'VVS Rossii' (Russian Air Force) titles

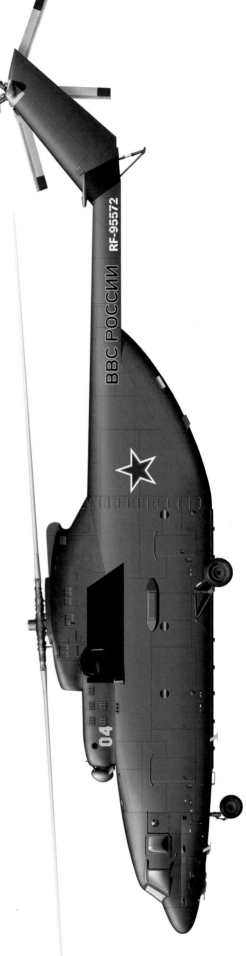

ВВС РОССИИ

RF-95572

Russian Air Force Mi-26 '04 Yellow'/RF-95572 in overall grey colours

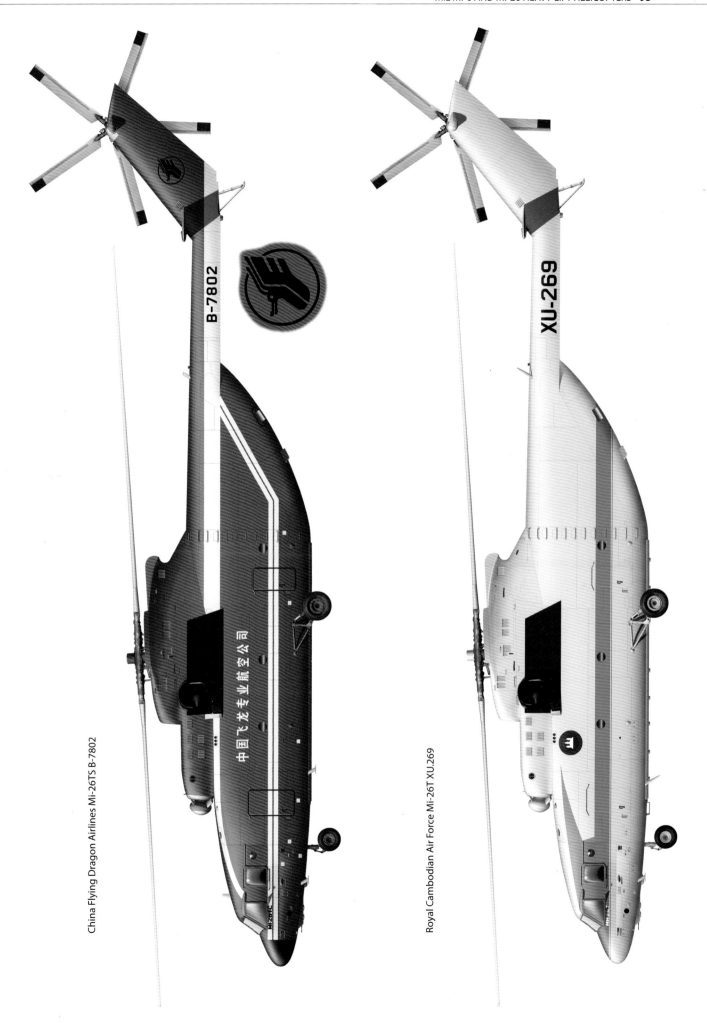

China Flying Dragon Airlines Mi-26TS B-7802

Royal Cambodian Air Force Mi-26T XU.269

Indian Air Force Mi-26 Z2898/B 'Zanskar' in its original two-tone camouflage

Democratic Republic of Congo Air Force Mi-26T 9T-HM15